Alte Nationalgalerie
Berlin

Prestel

Munich · London · New York

2nd revised edition, 2001
© 1997 by Prestel Verlag,
Munich · London · New York

© for illustrated works held by the artists
or their estates, with the exception of
works by Max Beckmann, Maurice
Denis, Ludwig von Hofmann, Aristide
Maillol, Claude Monet, Christian
Rohlfs, Max Slevogt: all held by VG
Bild-Kunst, Bonn, 1996, and Ernst
Ludwig Kirchner held by Dr. Wolfgang
and Ingeborg Henze, Wichtrach/Bern.

© of plans inside front and back covers:
H.G. Merz

Photographers: Christian Ahlers, Jörg P.
Anders, Reinhard Friedrich, Klaus
Göken, Andres Kilger, Bernd Kuhnert,
Karin März, Gerhard Murza, Werner
Zellien, Jens Ziehe, Central Archive of
the State Museums, all in Berlin.

Editor: Bernhard Maaz

Front Cover:
Adolph Menzel, *The Balcony Room*, 1845
(See p. 67)

Prestel Verlag
Mandlstrasse 26, 80802 Munich
Tel.: +49 (89) 38 17 09-0
Fax: +49 (89) 38 17 09-35;
4 Bloomsbury Place,
London WC 1A 2QA
Tel.: +44 (20) 7323-5004
Fax: +44 (20) 7636-8004;
175 Fifth Avenue, Suite 402,
New York, NY 10010
Tel.: +1 (212) 995-2720,
Fax: +1 (212) 995-2733

www.prestel.com

Translated from the German by
Fiona Elliott and Almuth Seebohm
Copyedited by: Jacqueline Guigui-
Stolberg

Design: zwischenschritt, Munich
Lithography: Fotolito Longo, Bozen
Typesetting: Mega-Satz-Service, Berlin
Printing and Binding: Passavia
Druckerei GmbH, Passau

Printed in Germany on acid-free paper
ISBN 3-7913-2624-4

Alte Nationalgalerie
Staatliche Museen zu Berlin
Stiftung Preußischer Kulturbesitz
Bodestrasse 1–3
10178 Berlin
Tel. +49 (30) 20 90 50 and 20 90 58 01
Fax +49 (30) 20 90 58 02 and
20 90 58 17

Opening hours
Tuesday – Sunday
10:00 a.m. – 6:00 p.m.
Thursdays 10:00 a.m. – 10:00 p.m.
Closed Mondays

**Museum Education and Visitor
Service**
For information on guided group tours:
Tel. +49 (30) 20 90 55 55
Fax +49 (30) 20 90 55 02

Public tours
Sundays at 11:00 a.m. (fortnightly)

Opinion Times
Paintings and sculptures appraised by
appointment on Wednesdays and Fridays
10 a.m. – 12 p.m.

Further information on the Staatliche
Museen zu Berlin–Stiftung Preußischer
Kulturbesitz is available at its Internet
website: www.smb.spk-berlin.de

If you are a regular visitor to the Alte
Nationalgalerie you may like to become
a member of the "Friends of the Nationalgalerie." Information on the many
advantages of membership may be had
from the:

**Verein der Freunde der
Nationalgalerie**
Rankestrasse 21
10789 Berlin
Tel +49 (30) 2 14 96 187
Fax +49 (30) 2 14 96 100

Contents

The Alte Nationalgalerie

The Name and the Building

The Alte Nationalgalerie situated on the Museumsinsel (Museum Island) houses one of the most important collections of nineteenth-century painting and sculpture, and since it was opened in 1876 it has been a fascinating monument to the history of the visual arts, politics, and culture of Germany.

The very name, "Alte Nationalgalerie" (Old National Gallery) is the outcome of recent political events, for since reunification Berlin is now blessed with two national galleries. In the Tiergarten district of West Berlin there is the Neue Nationalgalerie (New National Gallery), constructed by Mies van der Rohe in 1968, a masterpiece of modern architecture. Unification has in fact provided an opportunity to reorganize the national collection, and 20th century works will now be shown in the Mies van der Rohe building while contemporary art will be on view on a rotating basis in the Hamburger Bahnhof — Museum für Gegenwart (Museum for the Present), Berlin, which is situated halfway between the Alte Nationalgalerie and the Neue Nationalgalerie. Since Mies van der Rohe had the foresight to incorporate the name "Neue Nationalgalerie" into the design of the facade of his building in the Tiergarten, after unification the mother gallery on the Museumsinsel by definition became the "Alte Nationalgalerie." However, Mies van der Rohe did not only allude in his choice of name to the older gallery, for in his design of a temple on a podium he was clearly also using the same architectural language as that of the Alte Nationalgalerie. This was designed in 1865 by Friedrich August Stüler, a pupil of Karl Friedrich Schinkel's. After Stüler's death the building was then constructed according to his design by the court master builder Johann Heinrich Strack during the period 1866 to 1876. The idea of building a temple goes back to a design by King Friedrich Wilhelm IV. The king himself had a dilettante interest in architecture and was in fact a pupil of Schinkel's. After having created the Museumsinsel, his plan was that at its center there should be a building in the form of a classical temple set high on a podium, containing a lecture theater and a banqueting hall. The original inspiration was twofold: Schinkel's plan for a palace on the Acropolis in Athens (1834) and an earlier design from 1796 by his teacher, Friedrich Gilly, for a memorial to Frederick the Great in the form of a temple on a podium, detached from the everyday world by its elevated position.

Thus the Alte Nationalgalerie stands imposingly up above the colonnaded "sacred grounds" devoted to the arts and the muses on Berlin's Museumsinsel. While this lofty temple to the arts embodies the Romantic notion of a museum as an "aesthetic church," it also bears witness to the nation's love of grandeur and sense of itself during the *Gründerjahre* in late nineteenth-century Germany. Constructed entirely in Nebra sandstone at the then stupendous cost of three million marks, the Nationalgalerie has rightly been seen as a monument to the new-found wealth of Prussia and its claims to be the cultural leader of the German Empire. The extravagant, barely used, free-standing flight of steps is imposingly crowned by the mounted figure (made by Calandrelli to a design by Gustav Blaeser) of Friedrich Wilhelm IV, the Romantic on the throne of Prussia whose love of the arts inspired the founding of the Museumsinsel. Up above the figure of the King, a prominent inscription on the frieze — DER DEUTSCHEN KUNST 1871 (TO GERMAN ART 1871) — places the building in the context of the new political unity of the German nation achieved through the founding of the Reich, which came in 1871 during the ten years it took to construct the Alte Nationalgalerie. This inscription also underlines the gallery's role as a shrine dedicated to German art, with Germania personified as the patron saint of the arts on the pediment relief. On top of the pediment stand Rudolf Schweinitz's statues of the sister arts: painting, sculpture, and architecture.

View of the Alte Nationalgalerie, 1968

The History of the Collection

In view of the Alte Nationalgalerie's political and patriotic exterior ornament, which continues inside with Otto Geyer's stairwell frieze of German cultural history, and in view, too, of the celebration of the Prussian royal family as patrons of German art that this implies, it is perhaps surprising that the original collection was in fact donated by a commoner. In 1861 the Berlin banker and consul, Joachim Heinrich Wilhelm Wagener, left his collection of 262 nineteenth century paintings from Germany and elsewhere to Prince Wilhelm, later to become King and Emperor Wilhelm I. It was Wagener's express hope that the state would build on his collection "so that it might grow to become a national collection showing the continuing development of new painting." In this desire Wagener was clearly influenced by artists' demands — ever more persistent since the bourgeois uprising of 1848 — for state support in the shape of a national gallery which would purchase and collect contemporary art. With the acceptance of the Wagener bequest, Prussia now found itself in possession of the most comprehensive collection of contemporary art in Germany at that

time. Although the collection included some major works by Caspar David Friedrich, Schinkel, and Gaertner, it contained mainly bourgeois genre and history paintings from the main German art centers of the nineteenth century, concentrating on artists from Berlin, Düsseldorf, and Munich. But there were also examples of work by Austrian, Belgian, French, and Scandinavian painters. On accepting this bequest, the king then proceeded to enhance his own reputation by immediately adding contemporary works from his private collection. In addition, in order to lend weight to Prussian claims to leadership, he immediately decreed that the ceremonial building once planned by his brother Friedrich Wilhelm IV for the Museumsinsel should now be construct-

View of the Neue Nationalgalerie

ed to house the national collection. Thus this museum in fact prefigured the political unity that was not finally achieved until construction was already under way.

This also explains the subsequent enthusiasm for further bequests and purchases. It meant that Max Jordan, the gallery's first director — and a trained art historian — was able to buy Adolph Menzel's *Flute Concert* as well as his *Iron Rolling Mill* of 1875 immediately prior to the opening of the gallery. But although the latter was the gallery's most modern work at the time, neither it nor Jordan's other important purchases of works by Menzel, Böcklin, and Feuerbach, nor the bourgeois genre and history paintings of the Wagener bequest were the center of attraction at the ceremonial opening of the Nationalgalerie on the emperor's birthday on March 21, 1876. The spotlight was in fact on the two immense central rooms — which in those days were still two stories high — given over to cartoons by Peter Cornelius, monumental designs for his mythological and biblical wall frescos in Munich and Berlin. Given this position in the main rooms of the Nationalgalerie and honored with a more than life-sized bust in the apse, Cornelius — with his late Nazarene idealizing linear style, and who had been summoned to Berlin from Munich in 1840 — was thus held up as the prime exponent of art as favored by the imperial state at the time.

No sooner had the gallery opened than it was too small and the lack of space was only compounded by further purchases under the auspices of the "Landeskunstkommission" (Regional Art Commission), a state body dominated by professors from the Prussian art academies in Berlin, Düsseldorf, and Königsberg. This led to protracted arguments over the gallery's acquisitions policy. After Max Jordan had left, worn down by the struggle, this running dispute escalated under Hugo von Tschudi to the level of scandal. A few months after his appointment in 1896 as the director of the Nationalgalerie, Tschudi travelled with Max Liebermann to Paris

where he instantly bought, on behalf of the Nationalgalerie, Manet's *Conservatory,* a major work of French Impressionism. This was the opening move in Tschudi's subsequent breath-taking campaign to purchase modern French art, including works by Manet, Monet, Degas, Cézanne, Renoir, and Rodin — artists whose works were not as yet to be found in any other galleries.

The level of provocation that this induced may be measured against the inscription on the portico of the Nationalgalerie, which dedicated the building to German art while the date, 1871, linked the unification of the Reich with the defeat of the French. In Tschudi's view, however, this inscription meant that the Nationalgalerie should collect everything that was relevant to German art and, for him, this included modern French painting which he felt achieved its greatest heights in the work of Manet. In 1897 he boldly undertook the first reorganization of the collection. He grouped his new acquisitions in the rooms adjoining the Cornelius rooms, and, in doing so, started the transformation of the Nationalgalerie from a patriotic temple of the arts into an international art museum where the only criterium was quality.

Tschudi's transformation of the Nationalgalerie into a leading museum of modern art provoked a sharp reaction. Following the ensuing debate, which was even taken up in the Prussian parliament, in April 1899 Wilhelm II visited the Nationalgalerie. After his visit Wilhelm II decreed that the new acquisitions should not be displayed so prominently, that Tschudi's reorganization should be undone and that all future acquisitions and bequests should be subject to his own personal approval.

Far from being cowed by this imperial decree, Tschudi continued to purchase modern paintings, circumventing the Landeskunstkommission and its state budgetary controls with the help of private patrons, mostly art connoisseurs from among the Jewish upper classes. However, in order for the stocks that

Second Cornelius Room with a bust of Cornelius by August Wittig, before reconstruction, 1907

he was acquiring to be accepted by the gallery as gifts, Tschudi needed the emperor's approval. In fact, he managed to win the emperor's favor by putting on spectacular exhibitions such as the so-called "Centenary Exhibition of German Art" in 1906. This was the first time there had been an exhibition devoted to the particular achievements of German art, in this case between 1775 and 1875. It led to the rediscovery of German Romanticism; for the first time not only Caspar David Friedrich and Carl Blechen but also Leibl and the young Menzel received the recognition due to them, and outstanding examples of their work were purchased by Tschudi using state funds.

However, undermined by an intrigue instigated by the emperor, and hampered by ill will on the part of the gallery's "Generaldirektor," Wilhelm von Bode, in 1909 Tschudi moved to Munich as the director of the present Bayerische Staatsgemäldesammlungen (Bavarian State Collections of Paintings), taking with him all the paintings he had purchased on his own initiative, including major works by Van Gogh and Gauguin.

Now the emperor tried in vain to have his own art adviser, the history painter and director of the Berlin Academy, Anton von Werner, installed as the new director. Instead Tschudi's successor was Ludwig Justi, who proceeded to complete Tschudi's transformation of the Nationalgalerie from a "patriotic picture store" into an international art museum. Justi's reconstruction of the Nationalgalerie, which he described in a number of notes in 1910, consisted initially of a very practical series of divisions on the first floor. Behind the transverse hall, still today the ideal space for showing the collection of marble sculptures, there was a dark, awkward columned hall, which Justi then divided up into a series of smaller rooms. With decor ranging in style from Philipp Otto Runge through to touches of Art Nouveau, these rooms — today often wrongly taken to be original — were particularly suited to the middle-sized and more intimate format of works by Böcklin, Leibl, and Menzel. But Justi's administrative and conceptual reconstruction of the Nationalgalerie was much more sweeping. He saw to it that responsibility for the Nationalgalerie was transferred into the hands of the Prussian Ministry of Culture, in itself a body under parliamentary control. In addition, Justi managed to replace the notorious Landeskunstkommission, which consisted of artists who only ever approved purchases that complied with their own academic taste, with an acquisitions commission whose members were suitably knowledgeable about art history. Finally, Justi was able to relocate the collection's numerous patriotic history paintings and battle scenes to the State Armory and other military museums.

In 1919 Justi put on an exhibition of contemporary art in the Kronprinzenpalais (the crown prince's palace) in the avenue Unter den Linden, which was now empty after World War I and the consequent demise of the Prussian monarchy. On the upper floor were works by Van Gogh and a collection of the leading German Expressionists of the day. Hotly debated and attacked, even by Justi's contemporaries such as Max Liebermann and Karl Scheffler, the Nationalgalerie became the focus for the controversy surrounding modern art. In 1937 the discussion was abruptly brought to a halt by the National Socialists. The Nationalgalerie's contemporary holdings were confiscated as *"entartet"* or "decadent" and the crown prince's palace was closed. With the outbreak of war, it was not possible to

The Friedrichswerder Church (designed 1824 by Karl Friedrich Schinkel, completed 1830), view from the east, 1996

visit the Nationalgalerie after September 1, 1939. In 1940, the gallery's holdings were moved across Berlin into air-raid towers at the zoo and in Friedrichshain. In March 1945, four hundred of the best works were hidden in the Merkers mines in the Werra district and in Grasleben in the Harz mountains and were moved from there to the west after the war. Sculptures and large-scale paintings stayed in the cellars of the Nationalgalerie, which was itself partially destroyed in the last months of the war.

The Arrangement of the Gallery

Renovations to the Alte Nationalgalerie, including a lavishly redesigned entrance area, were carried out between 1998 and 2001. The building was carefully restored in keeping with its status as a listed historic monument. In the process, it was equipped with state-of-the-art air-conditioning and security systems as well as a modern infrastructure for visitors. The collection will profit enormously from the two spacious modern halls with daylighting now on the third floor. Major works by Caspar David Friedrich and Karl Friedrich Schinkel will be presented here.

The Berlin sculpture dating from the first half of the nineteenth century on display in the Friedrichswerder Church will be retained and expanded. Many of these works refer to Schinkel as the leading architect in Berlin. They are housed in one of Berlin's most beautiful interiors. The tour of the museum follows the route established by the provisional hanging made for the reopening of the Alte Nationalgalerie in 1998. It begins on the third floor with art from the Age of Goethe, in view of the Nazarene frescoes from the Casa Bartholdy in Rome which are installed there. Schadow's marble tomb of Count Alexander von der Mark is set up on the top flight of stairs. It is one of the major works of Neo-Classicism in Europe. On the third floor the focus is on art of the Romantic and Biedermeier periods.

On the second floor, or piano nobile, the French Impressionists are displayed on the visual axis of the middle rooms — just as Tschudi had once hoped. First, however, there is a middle room presenting the German painters in Rome, i.e. Böcklin, Feuerbach and Hans von Marées. In rooms leading off to the left and right are German artists inspired by the French, namely Leibl and his group on the left, and Liebermann and Uhde on the right. Works by the Salon painters and by different German schools illustrate the wide variety of contemporary styles between 1850 and 1880.

On the first floor the Neo-Classical sculptures in the Marble Hall represent an ideal contrasting with the Realist tendencies in painting from 1850 to the end of the century. At the beginning is Courbet, in the center the unparalleled rich Menzel collection. Works that satisfied official Wilhelmine tastes and paintings by the Berlin Secession artists round off the tour. Finally, with Rauch's *Victoria* still in sight, the Symbolism of the fin de siècle is illustrated by Max Beckman's *Small Death Scene* showing the influence of Edvard Munch. This juxtaposition combines the utopianism and the disillusionment of the 19th century.

Peter-Klaus Schuster
Director, Staatliche Museen zu Berlin

19th Century
Paintings and Sculptures

Contributors:

Andrea Bärnreuther   *AB*
Claude Keisch   *CK*

Bernhard Maaz   *BM*
Karin Schrader   *KS*
Birgit Verwiebe   *BV*
Angelika Wesenberg   *AW*

Johann Gottfried Schadow
(1764–1850)

Double statue of the princesses Luise
and Friederike of Prussia,
1795–97
Marble, 68 x 34 ½ x 23 ¼ in.
From the Stadtschloß, Berlin

The double statue of Crown Princess
Luise and Princess Friederike of Prussia
marks a highpoint in European Classi-
cism. For the first time, two female figures were portrayed life-size as a double
statue, that is to say, individuals were
being depicted who had no claims on
posterity by virtue of their achievements

as rulers or as military figures. Luise looks into the distance with patient resolve, viewing her future duties as queen. Friederike leans against her older sister's side. Dreamingly thoughtful yet coquettish, she takes her sister's hand resting on her shoulders in a gently sensitive gesture. The closeness of the two sisters and the contrast of their characters and destinies resonate equally in this graceful work.   *BM*

Johann Gottfried Schadow
(1764–1850)

Draped Female Figure,
c. 1811–17
Clay, fired, 13 x 5³/₄ x 4 in.
Acquired 1888 from Eugenie Schadow

A tall female figure turns her head over her shoulder, revealing her mature physical form. As a companion piece to this figure, Schadow made a contrasting figure of a youth at a sacrificial stone. Both figures are energetically formed, with similarly finely worked bodies and rather sketchier facial features, hands and curled hair: these parts would have been refined in the planned, but never executed, full-size versions. The rhythmic outlines of these two related figures are set against non-specific indications of drapery.   *BM*

Johann Gottfried Schadow
(1764–1850)

Resting Girl, 1826
Marble, 13¹/₄ x 37¹/₂ x 15 in.
Acquired 1865

When Schadow found himself practically without commissions in the 1820s, he created his *Resting Girl*. This statuette was not only to be his last work in marble, but was also to become a splendid résumé of his life's work, perfectly

Schadow made this utterly realistic, extremely plastic self-portrait he was still under thirty years old and yet was already one of the leading masters of his time in his capacity as Sculptor to the Prussian Court, having already triumphed in Rome and now carrying out large-scale commissions for the Brandenburg Gate and the Stadtschloß (City Palace). His self-portrait is a telling expression of his own youthful verve combined with an inspired mixture of blithe clarity, of resolute determination, of spiritual mobility, and of elemental, earthbound solidity.   *BM*

Johann Gottfried Schadow
(1764–1850)

Tombstone for Count Alexander von der Mark, 1788–90
Marble, 245 ¼ x 145 ¾ in.
On permanent loan from the Church Parish of Dorotheenstadt

Count Alexander von der Mark, an illegitimate son of Friedrich Wilhelm II of Prussia, died before he had reached maturity. His tombstone, of architectural dimensions, is layered vertically to create depth and tiered horizontally in a series of zones situated one above the other, all centering on the life-size figure of the sleeping youth. He has taken off his helmet and his sword is slipping from his hand. In keeping with the ideals of Lessing and Herder he is shown both at ease and at rest. A corner of the draperies leads the viewer's gaze down to a relief on the front side of the sarcophagus which shows Saturn wresting the youth from Minerva's hands and taking him off into the underworld. Meanwhile Minerva, the goddess of knowledge and of the skills of war, is trying to lure him back and send him instead towards a military future, symbolized in the shield and battle trophies. At either end, on the narrow sides of the sarcophagus, are the figures of Sleep and of Death, linking together short-lived and eternal sleep, life and death. Up above, in a shallow, semi-circular niche are the Three Fates, the goddesses who deter-

combining his artistic principles: quotation from classical antiquity — with a reference to the hermaphrodites of that era — and an even greater degree of lifelike Realism in the representation of the subject's material physicality, as for example in the virtually palpable softness of the skin. The angle of the girl's body creates a finely balanced interplay of relaxed appeal and cool withdrawal, a game of promise and denial.   *BM*

Johann Gottfried Schadow
(1764–1850)

Self-Portrait, c. 1790–94
Clay, fired, 16 x 8 ½ x 9 ¾ in.
Acquired 1917

Schadow looks at some imaginary other person with his mouth just barely open and his head inclined slightly forward. The herm-like, unclothed breast section is kept intentionally small and is thus timeless in its aspect. It is only by the bundle of hair at the nape of his neck that the artist may be placed in the late eighteenth century — the age of the ponytail. But, seen from the front, the locks of hair falling around his high forehead look perfectly natural. When

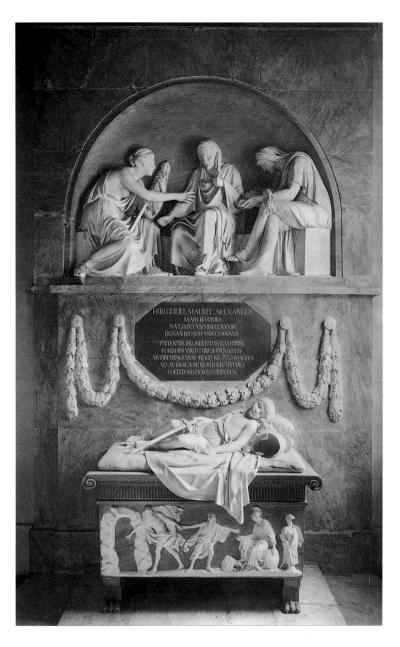

mine human destiny: the youthful Clotho spins the thread of life, the aged Atropos cuts it off — despite Clotho's attempts to prevent this — and Lachesis reads in the Book of Destiny. Thus human life and death alike are bound up in a higher order of fate which no individual can ever escape. *BM*

Antonio Canova
(1757–1822)

Hebe, 1796
Marble, 63 x 25 1/2 x 33 1/2 in.
Acquired 1878

As the cup bearer of the gods and herself the goddess of youth, Hebe treads gracefully down from the clouds. Embodying hospitable generosity, her gestures are feminine as she offers a goblet containing the elixir of eternal youth. The gently flowing movement of her body, all the more elegant for its fine marble skin, is arrested in the two containers, which, made from hard gleaming metal, both contrast with and emphasize the translucence of the marble. Hebe is clothed in finely gathered drapery that plays around her legs, accentuating rather than concealing her shape. Her upper body is that of a girl, its form only hinted at as though wearing some light garment. Canova's art comes at the end of a tradition in which the pleasing decorative aspect of the whole was valued above the effectiveness of individual parts, and when it was also still artistically acceptable to portray transitory, non-plastic notions such as floating and the wind, very much in the spirit of Baroque ideals of representation.

Around 1800 the sculptor Canova enjoyed the highest of reputations throughout Europe, for his figures did indeed personify the Age of Sentiment and Sensibility.

BM

Bertel Thorvaldsen
(1768–1844)

Eros with Anacreon, 1823
Marble,
20 3/4 x 26 3/4 x 2 3/4 in.
Acquired 1941

Thorvaldsen took the subject of this intimate relief, of which there are several almost identical replicas, from the forty-first song of Anacreon. In this the graying poet tells of the visit that the rain-soaked God of Love, Amor, paid him one night. Having warmed himself by the fire, Amor mischievously tests out his bow and arrow on his well-meaning host to see whether "the rain has not softened its sinews," and, having wounded the old poet with his arrow, then promptly leaves with a mocking verbal parting shot: "You see, my host, how lucky! / My arrow is undamaged / And soon your heart will sicken."

Thorvaldsen draws together the various themes of the poem, but concentrates on the moment of Amor's mischievous departure. His beautifully proportioned childish form is in full view while the old man with his laurel wreath and toga sits turned sideways on his bed. The work bears witness to Thorvaldsen's strict understanding of the relief as a form where powerful plasticity must clearly relate to the surface, where the formal clarity of the shapes is combined with intricate decorative detail, and where complete technical mastery serves his sensitivity to expressiveness.   *BM*

Alte Nationalgalerie, exhibition room with neoclassical sculptures

his own paintings and in his teachings and theoretical writings, he did much to establish the norms of neoclassicism as a creative principle. His proud self-portrait shows him in this double role, creating and teaching, holding his drawing tools in one hand while he gestures didactically with the other. He turns energetically and with the pride of the modern artist towards an unseen someone, yet his expansive gesture and the plasticity created by the steep angle of the light are nevertheless still reminiscent of Baroque traditions.   *BM*

Anton Raphael Mengs
(1728–1779)

Self-Portrait, c. 1773/74
Oil on wood, 35 $^1/_2$ x 29 $^1/_4$ in.
Acquired 1941

The Dresden court painter Mengs was a friend of Johann Joachim Winckelmann, the famous archaeologist. Mengs also lived and worked for many years in Rome where he was in daily contact with the artworks of antiquity. In both

Francisco José de Goya y Lucientes
(1746–1828)

The Maypole, c. 1808–12,
attributed to Goya
Oil on canvas, 32 $^1/_2$ x 40 $^3/_4$ in.
Acquired 1903, donation from Friedrich Alfred Krupp

Goya had already used the folkloric motif of the maypole once before in a tapestry design of 1787. Traditionally, bets would be placed and contestants would climb up the slippery pole to retrieve items of food. Now a quarter of

a century later, however, under the shadow both of his own darkening spirit and of the Spanish war of independence, the maypole is simply a vehicle for a crowd scene in a thundery half-light out of which looms a fortress-like house. In places, the paint has been applied with a spatula. Goya's late works are typified by such scenes of dark grandeur, by uneasy crowds, and by allusions to the power of the church (seen here in the crucifix on the bridge). However, his reliance on assistants and the rapid emergence of imitators mean that it is not certain that he carried this work out with his own hand.   *CK*

Anton Graff   (1736–1813)

Self-Portrait with Eye-shade, 1813
Oil on canvas, 25 1/2 x 20 in.
Acquired 1887

The Swiss-German portrait artist Anton Graff had already achieved success in Augsburg, Munich, and Regensburg by the time he was appointed court painter in Dresden in 1766. In 1789 he became Professor of Portraiture at the Academy there. His official position was that of portraitist to the aristocracy of Saxony, and with his deeply sensitive, virtually monochrome portraits of scholars, philosophers, and artists he became one of the most important portrait artists of the German Enlightenment. The new followers of the cult of friendship during the era of *Empfindsamkeit* (sentimentality) were beneficial to his genre. Two major collectors were commissioning work: Johann Wilhelm Ludwig Gleim commissioned portraits for his "Friendship Temple" in his house in Halberstadt while the Leipzig bookseller Philipp Erasmus Reich, following Gleim's lead, created a gallery of famous contemporary poets and thinkers. In Berlin in 1771, Graff made portraits of Moses Mendelssohn, Gotthold Ephraim Lessing, the poet Karl Wilhelm Ramler, and the philosopher and aesthete Johann Georg Sulzer, who became his father-in-law shortly afterwards. Sulzer was the author of a *General Theory of the Fine Arts* which accorded the portrait considerable importance.

As a mirror of the soul, portraiture took a leading position in the hierarchy of genres. Anton Graff himself estimated that he painted well over a thousand portraits. They reflect his development over a fifty-year period; starting with decorative baroque portraits he then, under the influence of Lavater and Sulzer, concentrated on the sitter's physiognomy before returning to full-length portraits around 1800. Graff painted self-portraits at every stage of his working life, well over fifty all told. His successful application for the position in Dresden in 1766 was in the form of a portrait, and even as late as 1813, the year he died, he still completed two self-portraits. His late portraits, carried out despite his failing sight, are astonishing in their freedom and intensity, and are more painterly in their conception than anything else hitherto.   *AW*

Gottlieb Schick (1779–1812)

Portrait of Heinrike Dannecker,
1802
Oil on canvas, 46 ¾ x 39 ½ in.
Acquired 1934

Heinrike Dannecker, the wife of the
Stuttgart court sculptor Dannecker, is seated parallel to the picture plane with an expansive landscape in the background. The broad sweep of the sitter's shape sets her apart from the infinitely vast, pale-blue cosmos. She turns towards the viewer in a wholly natural manner, and with her head raised, it is as though she welcomes this interruption in her thoughtful contemplation of nature and is inviting the intruder to share her pleasure. The flowers in her hand establish a link with nature. Yet this does not conceal the programmatic reference to contemporary events, with a clear allusion to the French tricolor in the colours of her clothes. Thus transient gesture, contemporary history, and the timelessness of the cosmos and nature come together and complement each other. *BM*

Eugène Delacroix (1798–1863)

Seated Nude
(Mademoiselle Rose),
c. 1820
Oil on canvas, 32 x 25 ½ in.
Acquired 1986

Delacroix drew and painted this model several times between 1817 and 1824. The square seat, the (unpainted) support for the raised arm, and the surrounding neutral darkness all show it to be a study for its own sake. Unimpressed by the clichés of antiquity, Delacroix investigated his model's physical appearance, paying particular attention to the mother-of-pearl sheen of her skin. A contemporary commentator on this work remarked that the young painter,

striving to emulate Rubens and Rembrandt, had discovered hitherto unknown planes and tones on his model and had declared to his friends that now he could paint! *CK*

Philipp Otto Runge (1777–1810)

Pauline Runge
with her two-year-old son,
Otto Sigismund, 1807
Oil on canvas, 38¼ x 28¾ in.
Acquired 1932, gift of Félicie Runge

Runge painted this portrait in 1807, three years after his marriage to Pauline Bassenge. Both his realistic view of his subjects and his treatment of the landscape demonstrate his search for a new formal language. Pauline, with their two-year-old son, Sigismund, on her arm, is stern and dignified in her aspect. The artist may have been stylistically influenced here by late Gothic sculptures of the Madonna, while the unfinished landscape in the background reflects Runge's Romantic notions of nature. *BV*

Caspar David Friedrich
(1774–1840)

Monk by the Sea, 1808–10
Oil on canvas, 43 1/4 x 67 1/2 in.
From the Berliner Stadtschloß

Friedrich worked for two years on this, ultimately his most famous work. The composition is divided horizontally into land, sea, and sky with a clear simplicity that shocked his contemporaries. A monk stands, bareheaded, on the shore. Seagulls circle around him. The lonely figure faces the leaden blackness of the immeasurably vast sea. The grey band of cloud over the water surprisingly gives way to blue sky along the top edge of the picture. No artistic composition had ever been as uncompromising as this: the main space of the picture seems like an abyss of some kind; there are no boundaries, there is nothing to hold on to, just a sense of floating between night and day, between despair and hope. In 1810 Heinrich von Kleist put into words, as no other could, the magical fascination of this painting: "Nothing could be more sombre nor more disquieting than to be placed thus in the world: the one sign of life in the immensity of the kingdom of death, the lonely center of a lonely circle. With its two or three mysterious objects the picture seems somehow apocalyptic, like Young's *Night Thoughts*, and since its monotony and boundlessness are only contained by the frame itself, contemplation of this picture gives one the sense that one's eyelids have been cut away."   BV

Caspar David Friedrich
(1774–1840)

Abbey among Oak Trees, 1809–10
Oil on canvas, 43 1/2 x 67 1/4 in.
From the Berliner Stadtschloß

Abbey among Oak Trees is the companion piece to *Monk by the Sea*. Friedrich showed both paintings in the Berlin Academy Exhibition of 1810. At the request of the 15-year-old crown prince, they were bought by King Friedrich Wilhelm III. In their perplexing remoteness and formal radicalism they were to become key works in German Romanticism. In *Monk by the Sea* a human being stands lost in the apocalyptic loneliness and infinity of nature and the cosmos. He meditates on life and its boundaries. In the companion piece, the gates of death have opened. Monks carry a coffin into a deserted Gothic ruin to hold a requiem mass under the cross. The graveyard with its crooked, sunken tombstones is equally deserted. Bare oaks reach up into the sky as though in complaint. The first light of dawn is appearing over the hori-

zon like an ocher-yellow veil, outshining the tender curve of the crescent moon. The visionary gleam of the heavenly realm is completely detached from the earthly regions, which are still sunk in darkness. One sign of hope is in the two single lights on the crucifix. For the painter Carl Gustav Carus, who was also a friend of Friedrich's, this painting was "of all recent landscapes, possibly the most deeply poetic work of art."

BV

calm, and mystery. To the left there are trees, but only with sparse foliage. To the right a bridge leads towards a small group of houses with smoke coming from the chimneys. In Friedrich's own words: "When a scene is shrouded in mist, it seems greater, nobler, and heightens the viewer's imaginative powers, increasing expectation — like a veiled girl. Generally the eye and the imagination are more readily drawn by nebulous distance than by what is perfectly plain for all to see."

In this work Friedrich both adopts and freely adapts the forms of nature, combining fields, trees, bridges, houses, and hills to create a landscape that only bears a general resemblance to the Elbe Valley near Dresden.

BV

Caspar David Friedrich
(1774–1840)

Mist in the Valley of
the Elbe, c. 1821
Oil on canvas, 13 x 16 3/4 in.
Since 1934 in the Nationalgalerie

A hilly landscape is shrouded in thick banks of mist. Seemingly damp fields and whitish mist reflect the rising sun. There is a sense of early morning freshness,

Caspar David Friedrich (1774–1840)

Morning in the Riesengebirge,
1810–11
Oil on canvas, 42½ x 67 in.
From the Berliner Stadtschloß

In the summer of 1810, Friedrich and his friend Georg Friedrich Kersting went on a walking tour in the Riesengebirge. The landscape moved Friedrich. Shortly afterwards he started work on this painting. After a visit to the artist's studio, Karl Friedrich Frommann wrote: "Plans for another large land-scape from the Riesengebirge in Silesia. The viewpoint is high in the mountains where a female figure by a cross at the highest peak is drawing the artist up towards herself; the lower slopes are to be almost entirely obscured by clouds while a ray of sunshine cuts through, lighting up the cross and the man."

In 1811 Friedrich showed the work at the Dresden Art Exhibition. The *Journal des Luxus und der Moden* (The Journal of Luxury and Fashions) hailed it as a "jewel of the exhibition." Only a year later Friedrich Wilhelm III bought it at

the Berlin Academy Exhibition. When he looked at the picture, he is supposed to have said: "Those who have not experienced this for themselves in nature would not believe it to be true." The newspaper *Die Vossische Zeitung* was already observing similarities between this work and Friedrich's seascapes. From its position on a rock in the foreground, the crucifix alone rises above the line of the horizon. Stretching out into the distance, the mountains lie like waves in the mist. A woman with blonde hair and a white dress has just reached the

peak of the rock in the foreground. With one hand on the crucifix, she is reaching down with the other to the man below — the artist himself — demonstrating the affinity of Friedrich's ideas to those of the early Romantics Schlegel and Schleiermacher, according to whom the loved-one leads the way to God. After *Cross in the Mountains* of 1807–08 (Staatliche Kunstsammlungen, Dresden, also known as *Tetschener Altar*), this is Friedrich's most important crucifix landscape.   *BV*

Caspar David Friedrich
(1774–1840)

Solitary Tree, 1822
Oil on canvas, 21 1/2 x 28 in.
Acquired 1861, Consul Wagener bequest

In 1822 the art patron and collector, Heinrich Wagener, commissioned a "times of day" diptych from Friedrich. The morning picture became *The Solitary Tree*. A grassy landscape with groups of trees, ponds, and villages extends to the foothills of the mountains behind the spires of a Gothic town. One mighty oak stands like a statue in the middle of the composition. A shepherd shelters beneath it. Its great trunk has withstood wind and weather, but the tips of the branches of this giant tree have already died off. Above the tree, the clouds form of a kind of cupola. Transgressing against the classical laws of composition, Friedrich cuts through all the various levels of the picture with the tree as the central foreground axis. And thus, at a stroke the oak tree takes on the role of mediator between heaven and earth, between the transcendental and the mundane. As an image of nature, it embodies natural strength and the life force, while at the same time the withered branches point to a life beyond this one.   *BV*

Caspar David Friedrich
(1774–1840)

Moonrise over the Sea, 1822
Oil on canvas, 21 3/4 x 28 in.
Acquired 1861, Consul Wagener bequest

Like its companion piece, the evening picture of the diptych was painted in 1822. In *Moonrise on the Seashore* Friedrich took up one of his favorite themes. In the reflected light of the night sky, it is as though the surface of the water begins to glow all of its own accord, taking up the light of heaven, as it were. Clouds have come up and the round shape of the full moon is half hidden behind the banks of cloud at the horizon. This means that the moonlight does not fall evenly but seems to be breaking out of a gateway in the clouds, creating a magical play of light. Complementary colours, ranging from golden to whitish yellow, violet and blue, define the contrasts of light and shade. There is a sense of the magnitude and

unity of the universe. Moved by this wonder of nature, three people sit on rounded rocks near the shore, and their dark silhouettes heighten the effect of the gleaming light of the sky and the sea. Two sailing ships pursue a ghostly course across the water. The sublime drama with the moon as the symbol of hope is imbued with a quality of unearthly beauty.   *BV*

celestial light of the moon that permeates the atmosphere with a festive stillness. Deep in the moonlit night the trees and rocks acquire strange, almost eerie, dimensions and importance. The two figures are united by their shared experience of the natural world confronting them with an awareness of their transience; together they face the mystery of the unfathomable. The date of origin of this painting is disputed; various dates between 1818 and 1835 have been proposed.   *BV*

Caspar David Friedrich
(1774–1840)

Man and Woman contemplating the Moon, 1824
Oil on canvas, 13 1/2 x 17 1/4 in.
Acquired 1935

Pausing on their nocturnal walk through a mountain forest is a couple on a rise beside a dramatically contorted, uprooted oak. Darkness envelops the strollers; their eyes are raised to the reassuring

Caspar David Friedrich (1774–1840)

Woman at a Window, 1822
Oil on canvas, 17 1/4 x 14 1/2 in.
Acquired 1906 from the family of the artist

A young woman stands at the window of Friedrich's studio. It is Caroline, the painter's wife. With her back to the viewer, she is looking out across the River Elbe to the other side. The bare interior of the studio is composed of strict horizontals and verticals. It seems lifeless and unlived-in. The only signs of life are the figure of the woman, the sight of the delicate green of the poplar trees, and the wide springtime sky. In this work, Friedrich has adopted a favorite theme of Romanticism, where the framework of a window links proximity and distance and evokes a longing for the unknown. The outward gaze, contemplating nature, also turns inwards towards the individual's own spiritual center.

BV

Caspar David Friedrich
(1774–1840)

Riesengebirge,
c. 1830–35
Oil on canvas, 28 1/4 x 40 in.
Acquired 1909

The gentle gradations of
the hills form a hollow that
is mirrored in the layers of
cloud in the sky. Heaven
and earth seem to merge
into an ellipse centered on
the soft violet range of
mountains in the distance. In the foreground, barely distinguishable in the
natural surroundings, a shepherd or a
walker sits on a rise, lost in his contemplation of the extent of this mountain
world. In 1810, Friedrich went on a
walking tour in the Riesengebirge with
his friend Kersting and made numerous
sketches which he continued to use as
studies for paintings into his old age. It
seems likely that this picture shows the
view from the "Koppenplan" southwest
towards the "Ziegenrücken." In this
landscape, early Romantic thinking and
religiosity come together, addressing the
sense of inner turmoil felt by many since
the Enlightenment, people who — in
the face of nature and its eternal cycles
— become all too aware of their isolation and yet nevertheless try, in medita-
tive contemplation, to become one with
the cosmos.   *KS*

was fired by enthusiasm for the days
when knights roamed the land, the
emotions aroused by twilight and night-
time, and dramatic lighting conditions.
Sharing the same enthusiasms, Carl
Borromäus von Miltitz had restored a
fortress once inhabited by his ancestors,
which was situated between Dresden
and Meißen. After 1812 he gathered a
circle of Romantic artists there. Their
dream is symbolized in the shape of the
knight on horseback springing towards
the newly revived fortress. Thus the
carefully executed, topographically exact
Burg Scharfenberg constitutes an amalga-
mation of a realistic view and a Romantic landscape. It seems that Oehme had
already drawn this same fortress from
memory in Rome in 1824. His friend
Ludwig Richter described the (now
lost) pen-and-ink drawing in his
memoirs: "An old castle with high
Renaissance gables, looking out from
among ancient, leafless oak trees and
showing a row of festively lit windows."
                                         AW

Ernst Ferdinand Oehme
(1797–1855)

Burg Scharfenberg at
Night, 1827
Oil on canvas, 23 1/4 x 32 3/4 in.
Acquired 1923

Oehme, a pupil of Caspar
David Friedrich's, stayed
faithful to his teacher's
themes and motifs all his
life, but never aspired to the
same spiritual heights. He

Carl Gustav Carus (1789–1869)

Balcony Room with a View of the Bay of Naples, c. 1829–30
Oil on canvas, 11 ¼ x 8 ½ in.
Property of the Verein der Freunde der Nationalgalerie

In 1828 the painter and physician, Carl Gustav Carus, accompanied Prince Friedrich August of Saxony to Italy. In his travel diary he described their arrival in Naples. He had been anticipating his quarters in the Casino Reale on the Via Chiatamone with mounting excitement: "At last I enter, and in front me lie Vesuvius, the sea, the castle, and the blue distance." Deeply impressed, he painted this view from his room of the harbor and the Castel dell'Ovo. The immediacy of the experience is intermingled with Romantic symbolism in the ambivalence of the external and internal world.   BV

Carl Gustav Carus
(1789–1869)

Pilgrim in a Rocky Valley, c. 1820
Oil on canvas, 11 x 8 ½ in.
Acquired 1924

"The pilgrim will recall to us the idea of distance, the very immeasurability of the earth's surface; but it will always be the landscape that determines the living being" — Carus's own words about landscape painting in a letter of 1820. The pilgrim is walking through the night, along the dark valley towards the morning star. Carus had drawn on themes such as this since becoming friends with Caspar David Friedrich. But, besides being influenced by Friedrich's thinking, Carus's works are clearly in tune with the wider Romantic *Zeitgeist*. Quite similar images occur, for example, in Ludwig Tieck's novel *Franz Sternbalds Wanderungen* (1798).   AW

Georg Friedrich Kersting
(1785–1847)

Outpost Duty, 1815
Oil on canvas, 18 x 13³/₄ in.
Acquired 1921

Kersting painted this picture as a memorial to three friends who had fallen in the Napoleonic wars: Theodor Körner, Karl Friedrich Friesen, and Heinrich Hartmann. Kersting had also followed Körner's lead and joined the Lützower Freikorps (volunteers) in 1813. As an unmounted marksman, "Jäger zu Fuß," Kersting had been given weapons and money by Kügelgen and Caspar David Friedrich. Goethe had pronounced the blessing of the arms. The painting represents both Kersting's patriotism and his grief. The three friends have taken up their position at the edge of an oak wood. They are wearing the Iron Cross medal, which was designed by Schinkel in 1813. Oak trees, their hair styles, and their red, black, and gold uniforms point towards a newly-awakened sense of being German. Silence reigns. Each member of the group seems lost in his own thoughts as though he were no longer of this world. Friesen leans against an oak tree with his rifle at the ready. As a drill instructor he fought alongside Friedrich Ludwig Jahn and became Lützow's personal adjutant. On the left of the picture sits Hartmann, a

nineteen-year-old law student from Heidelberg who had fought with Friesen and Kersting in the battle at Göhrde. Kersting was to see him die. The poet and dramatist Körner, sitting behind Hartmann, recruited volunteers for the Freikorps in Dresden. In his works, he advocated that the freedom of the fatherland should take precedence over the life of the individual.   *BV*

Georg Friedrich Kersting
(1785–1847)

The Wreath Maker, 1815
Oil on canvas, 15³/₄ x 12¹/₂ in.
Acquired 1921

Kersting painted this as a companion piece to *Outpost Duty*. A girl in white sits, withdrawn into herself, making wreaths by a group of oaks. Three oaks, with the names of the fallen Lützow riflemen carved into their trunks, stand behind her like tombstones. She has already woven two of the wreaths and the oak leaves for the third are ready beside her. Oak leaves had symbolized heroism since the eighteenth century. Kersting creates an intimate, inward-looking atmosphere in this work. The wood is like a temple with the grieving girl in front of it, making wreaths in memory of the heroes of the Fatherland.   *BV*

Karl Friedrich Schinkel
(1781–1841)

Morning, 1813
Oil on canvas, 30 x 40 in.
Acquired 1911, gift of Bruno Cassirer

Two women are walking with their children towards a grove of beech trees. The morning light falls at an angle through lush foliage, behind which the sun has already risen. Children play happily on the grass and two riders appear at the right-hand edge of the grove, dressed, as are the walkers, in Renaissance costume. The viewer's gaze is drawn irresistibly into the distance past ancient, overgrown fragments of stonework. The horizon broadens out into the sea where a port on the left has domes in the style of the Italian Renaissance. As so often in Schinkel's work, this landscape is as much historical as topographical. In his remembrance of the great epochs of the past, Schinkel evokes his vision of present social renewal. Painted in 1813 during the Napoleonic wars, the picture conveys a sense of renewed patriotism. Echoing Runge's *Times of Day*, Schinkel painted a companion piece entitled *Evening* which was, however, destroyed in 1945. In that work, the struggle against Napoleon was symbolized by two eagles hovering during a storm above a rock surrounded by oak trees. Both works were commissioned by General von Gneisenau and reflect his wish that together they should herald the dawn of a new age following a night of stormy darkness.   *BV*

Karl Friedrich Schinkel
(1781–1841)

View of the Flower of Greece,
1825 (Copy by Wilhelm Ahlborn, 1836)
Oil on canvas, 37 x 92 ¹/₂ in.
Acquired 1954

Against the background of an ideal Greek townscape, naked heroes are constructing an Ionic temple with a double row of columns. The motif of the procession on the frieze of the temple is of reminiscent of that the Parthenon. The painting captures the moment when the last marble block of the frieze is being heaved into position with a considerable expenditure of effort. The block has come from a temporary workshop where work on other sculptures is already under way. Schinkel's design for the columns goes back to earlier examples from antiquity. It is possible that he was influenced by engravings (owned by his teacher Friedrich Gilly) of Hadrian's Villa in Tivoli. The Greek inscription to the left on the temple wall quotes Aristotle's hymn to the virtues of battle and to death on the battlefield. The men working by this inscription have stopped for a moment and are looking towards where soldiers are returning from war.

As in other works, Schinkel is alluding here to the Napoleonic wars and Prussia's struggle for independence. In addition there are also thoughts of Greece breaking free from Turkish rule, which had almost been achieved at the time when this picture was painted. This programmatic piece by Schinkel reveals both his view of the world and of art: "The landscape shows the great cultural wealth of a highly cultivated people who understand how to use everything in nature in order to win from it a higher level of life both for the individual and for the people in general." In his view, the construction of a temple was the crowning glory of an ordered society and symbolic of an improved world order.

In his vision of a new Athens, Schinkel was referring to his own architectural project in Berlin to create an Athens on the Spree river. In his designs for the columned hall of the museum at the Lustgarten, he employed the same stylistic means as in this temple. Similarly, the monument in the central plane in depth is clearly reminiscent of Albert Wolff's lion fighter and August Kiß's Amazon which decorate the stairs of the Altes Museum.

Schinkel's original version of this painting has been lost. However, it was preserved for posterity by Wilhelm Ahlborn who copied it in 1826 and again in 1836. *BV*

Karl Friedrich Schinkel
(1781–1841)

Gothic Church on a Rock
by the Sea, 1815
Oil on canvas, 28 1/4 x 38 1/2 in.
Acquired 1861, Consul Wagener bequest

It is dusk and a group of riders is moving towards the sea, most probably to embark in the harbor. The wind coming up from the sea tugs at their clothes and violently shakes the trees and the bushes. The scene is almost completely in darkness with the setting sun hidden behind the Gothic church that rises up majestically on a rock right by the water, as though it had originally formed as part of the natural rock. The transition from land to sea is like a cliff there, and the house of God seems like a vision bathed in an auspicious glow, a telling image of the Christian world view. Schinkel's leaning towards narrative and drama shows his close affinity with the poets of German Romanticism such as Clemens Brentano and Achim von Arnim, whose influence accounted for Schinkel's preference for old German themes and medieval architecture in his works. In those days, it was generally thought that the Gothic style was German in origin, which in itself explains the enthusiasm among the Romantics for that period and its architecture, particularly during the period 1813 to 1815 with its groundswell of patriotism.   *BV*

house reports: "The question arose as to the difficulty of expressing in a drawing what could be so easily achieved through poetry. Schinkel refuted this and Brentano wanted to prove that he could easily improvise a narrative on the spot that Schinkel would by no stretch of the imagination be able to keep up with or adequately express through drawing. After much discussion to and fro, and after the length of any such narrative had been agreed, it was decided — to the company's loud delight — that the two should be put to the test. Brentano spoke and Schinkel drew." Brentano's story was about an old castle-like hunting lodge in which a head forester, now dead, had once lived. Because the ground was so rocky, he was buried on the other bank of the river. And now a deer could safely come into the grounds of the deserted castle. Schinkel's painting perfectly conveyed the complicated structure of Brentano's narrative. As in the narrative, there are various layers of meaning in the painting with the symbols of a religious-Romantic worldview in the crucifix, church, burial, dove, wine, and children. But the transience of all things earthly as well as the idea of nature reclaiming the world also find formal expression in this painting which the art collector Consul Wagener commissioned from Schinkel on the basis of two drawings he made during the contest.   *BV*

Karl Friedrich Schinkel
(1781–1841)

Castle by the River, 1820
Oil on canvas, 27 $^1/_2$ x 37 in.
Acquired 1861, Consul Wagener bequest

This fairy tale piece was the result of an artists' contest between Karl Friedrich Schinkel and Clemens Brentano. Carl Gropius, one of the guests at a certain soirée in Schinkel's

The Friedrichswerder Church, view of the interior with classical sculptures

The Friedrichswerder Church

As both architect and town planner, Schinkel's influence on the face of Berlin was varied and enduring, yet war and subsequent reconstruction schemes have meant that there are now relatively few of his buildings left that still have their original interior and exterior. Even his most magnificent creation, the Altes Museum, has been radically altered inside, with the exception of the rotunda — all of which accounts for the particular significance of the Friedrichswerder Church (completed in 1830) in that it perfectly demonstrates Schinkel's aims and intentions. Although the taste of his royal client restricted Schinkel's choice of form for the church, which is based on the Gothic style, he had free reign when it came to the materials to be used. This church is one of the first post-Baroque buildings where brick — produced in Germany in the middle ages and thus imbued with patriotic sentiment — is conspicuously employed. Shortly afterwards brick was again used for the neighboring Building Academy, which in itself was to constitute the

first example of a floor plan following the pragmatic approach of the most advanced English industrial architecture of the time.

On display in the Friedrichswerder Church, besides documentation about Schinkel's life and work, there are also sculptures by his colleagues and contemporaries. These include statues of artists from the Altes Museum, monumental sculpture — for example from the tomb of Queen Luise of Prussia by Rauch, architectural sculptures like Schadow's and Tieck's works for the Stadtschloß (City Palace), and other uncommissioned works. As the king's favored architect, Schinkel was able to pass on many commissions to his friends and contemporaries working in sculpture.

BM

Christian Friedrich Tieck
(1776–1851)

Karl Friedrich Schinkel, 1819
Marble, 26 1/4 x 15 x 10 1/2 in.
Acquired 1923

The period after the Napoleonic wars was marked by numerous architectural projects; the leading figures of the age, such as Wilhelm von Humboldt, Christian Daniel Rauch, and Tieck also notably included Schinkel who, after his beginnings as a set designer and painter, had already created his first architectural showpiece in the form of the Neue Wache (a surveillance building). In 1821, Schinkel's reconstruction of the Berlin Schauspielhaus (Berlin Theater) was completed with architectural ornamentation by Tieck, a protégé of Goethe's at the time, in a manner in keeping with the architect's own classical style. Further testimony to the friendship between Schinkel and Tieck may be found in Tieck's portrait bust of Schinkel from 1819. The portrait combines the markedly individual features of the architect with a timelessly classical breast piece. Thus the lifelike quality of the portrait with the realistic, strong movement of the head is linked with an idealized claim to lasting fame. Since it first went on show, this bust has always counted as the best portrayal both of Schinkel's physiognomy and of his immense creativity. *BM*

Unknown sculptors after designs by Karl Friedrich Schinkel
(1781–1841)

Reliefs from the Building Academy in Berlin, 1832
Clay, fired, each picture space 15 3/4 x 32 3/4 x 5 1/2 in.

At one time located directly next to the Friedrichswerder Church, the Building Academy, constructed between 1831 and 1836 was, along with the Schauspielhaus and the Altes Museum, one of Schinkel's most important buildings. It gained prominence even before it was finished. It was the first building to show the influence of the latest industrial architecture from England. The floor plan allowed flexibility in the positioning of the walls. The walls themselves were constructed according to a pattern of simple repeated elements. The material (brick) was made in Germany. The sculptural ornamentation, in particular the reliefs below the window ledges on the main floor, represented programmatically the function of the building at that time as the Building Academy, portraying the history of building since antiquity and the various activities it involves.

BM

Emil Wolff (1802–1879)

Nymph, 1868, model 1836
Marble, 61 x 23 x 18 3/4 in.
Acquired 1949

Although this nymph belongs to Wolff's
late period, it is nevertheless a perfect
example of the particular quality of his
strictly classical approach to art that he
had developed as far back as the 1830s,
where the ideal subject almost becomes
a genre piece while the whole is carried
out with consummate technical mastery.
The even distribution of weight creates
an impression of timeless peace; classical
draperies shield the noble form. Fore-
runners from antiquity with drapery
drawn similarly over one shoulder are
of no more than secondary importance.
Despite lending his works an air of
antiquity, Wolff retained his own artistic

independence and integrity in such a
way that particularly befits his works
with their classical lines.   *BM*

Emil Wolff (1802–1879)

Amor, the Conqueror of Strength,
1835–36
Marble, 54 3/4 x 21 1/4 x 18 3/4 in.
Acquired 1949

Much in demand and admired as a classical sculptor, Wolff was both a pupil and
a nephew of Schadow's. All his life he
worked in Rome where there were
more potential buyers. Many of his
sculptures, mostly idealized in their subject matter, were made in marble several
times over and usually went to buyers
from the aristocracy in Europe and
America. Wolff's success was due to his

artistic ability plus his deep knowledge of and feeling for antiquity, in conjunction with his unusually appealing subject matter and his first-class training in the techniques of sculpture. There can be no better example of this than his life-size Amor, the god of love. With his youthful freshness and boyish, longingly expectant gaze, Amor holds Hercules' cudgel, a symbol of strength, alluding to the omnipotence of love. This also explains the earlier title of the piece: Amor as the Conqueror of the Globe. Thus Wolff does not see Amor as the provocative god of erotic sensuality and desire still typical of the late eighteenth century, but instead imbues him with a greater degree of seriousness and philosophical depth.   *BM*

Ridolfo Schadow
(1786–1822)

Woman Spinning,
1816–18
Marble,
49 1/4 x 30 1/4 x 26 3/4 in.
Acquired 1949

This figure has a lightness about it that comes equally from its subject matter, the upwards flow of the composition, the contrast of the graceful movement of the body with the solidly immovable block of stone, and the fluid treatment of the youthful female form and its draperies. Any impression of playfulness is, however, dispersed by the elegance of her absorption in the task in hand, and by the mimetic and gestural conciseness of the form as opposed to its surroundings. While earlier generations might have understood a woman spinning as a symbol for the Three Fates, spinning and ultimately cutting through the

thread of human life, here Ridolfo Schadow — very much in the manner of his teacher Thorvaldsen — is focusing on the moment when the whole looks more like a genre piece that seems to have been rendered timeless by the classically-trained eye. The outstanding success of Schadow's works was the result of his perfectly satisfying the lyrical quality of contemporary taste.   *BM*

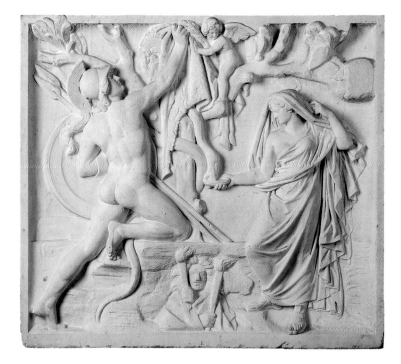

Christian Daniel Rauch
(1777–1857)

Jason and Medea, 1805–10, 1818
Marble, 48 1/2 x 55 in.
From the Rauch Museum

Rauch's unfinished relief depicts the
scene from the tale of the Argonauts
when Jason takes the golden fleece from
Colchis, where King Aeëtes had been
keeping it. The king's daughter fell in
love with Jason and helped him in his
mission by administering a magic potion
to the hundred-eyed dragon that was
guarding the fleece. The relief shows
the moment when Amor, the god of
love, is handing the fleece down from a
tree. Hecate, the goddess of magic, plays
her part from the underworld and
ensures Jason's success. The image is
dominated by the contrast between the
main figures: the athletic warrior with
his lance, shield, and helmet, reaching
out confidently and energetically for the
prized treasure, as opposed to the tender
young princess. Rauch combines two
consecutive acts, the administering of

the potion and the taking of the fleece,
into one moment, giving the whole the
impression of simultaneity. The reference
to themes from antiquity, as well as to a
successful statue of Jason that Thorvaldsen had made not long before, plus the
fact that this was not a commissioned
work, all show that first and foremost
Rauch wanted this work to demonstrate
his creative powers and that, at the same
time, he wanted to measure himself as
much against the sculptors of antiquity as
against one of the most highly esteemed
sculptors of his day.   *BM*

Christian Daniel Rauch
(1777–1857)

Seated Victoria, Throwing a Wreath,
1838–45
Marble, 87 3/4 x 41 3/4 x 35 1/2 in.
From the Stadtschloß, Berlin

This life-size figure of Victoria throwing a laurel wreath to the victor used to
be in the White Room in the Stadtschloß, halfway along one of the shorter

walls, symbolizing Prussia's military might. In the liveliness of its movement and in its air of graceful and timeless lightness, the light-footed form of the winged goddess of victory contrasts with the sentiment-laden, patriotic aspirations of its noble place of keeping. The form of the figure goes back to one of the Victorias that Rauch made for the Walhalla near Regensburg.   *BM*

Theodor Kalide   (1801–1863)

Bacchante on a Panther, 1844–48
Marble, fragment, c. 28 x 48 x 20 in.
Acquired 1878

This work was severely damaged in the war and is now without various important sections such as the arms, the plinth, and the animal's legs. But even as just a torso, the Bacchante lying face upwards on a panther shows, in the varied rhythm of its swelling, driving forms, the sheer excitement of the original composition of this piece. As the handmaids of Dionysus, the god of wine, the Bacchantes of ancient mythology accompanied their god each year on his ecstatic celebratory procession through nature. Euphoric with wine and unable to control their limbs, they would enter into a state where the usual limits of strict morality were quite forgotten. A panther, traditionally a

member Bacchus' retinue, provides a resting place for the Bacchante who jokes with him and hands him a bowl of nectar. Thus the interplay with the tamed animal bears witness to a pure affirmation of unfettered, sensual physicality.   *BM*

Frescos from the Casa Bartholdy (1816–17)

Johann Friedrich Overbeck (1789–1869)

The Selling of Joseph
Fresco on plaster, 95 3/4 x 119 3/4 in.
Acquired 1887

Peter Cornelius (1783–1867)

Joseph Interpreting Dreams
Fresco on plaster, 97 x 130 1/2 in.
Acquired 1887

Joseph Reveals Himself to His Brothers
Fresco on plaster, 93 x 114 1/4 in.
Acquired 1887

The wall paintings in the Casa Bartholdy were the first opportunity that the artists, initially mocked as "Nazarenes," had to work as they wanted in accordance with their own concept of art. Creating frescos in the style of the old Italian masters, depicting scenes from the Old Testament, and working as a group: all these elements were eminently compatible with the artistic and ethical ideals of the Nazarenes. The Prussian Consul General in Italy, Jakob Salomon Bartholdy, had put the banqueting room in his private residence at their disposal and provided them with paint and food so that the young artists, whose ideals he was familiar with, could rediscover the almost lost technique of fresco painting and realize their dream of a new form of art: monumental, jointly-created wall paintings. The individual scenes of the fresco, important moments in the story of Joseph, are independent of each other, differing both in the light and in the scale of the figures.

Peter Cornelius: "This work makes me the happiest of people, and even if I only had one crust of bread left, I would not change it … In my breast there beats a sure, prophetic feeling that art will break through from here to a new, beautiful existence." The two frescos by Cornelius are the finest of the series. Overbeck's work is less dramatic, although the theme of his picture is of central significance in that it shows the selling of Joseph by his jealous brothers, and thus explains subsequent events.

Bartholdy had the artists make sketches of the finished frescos so that he could convince the Prussian king of the skill of the young painters in Rome. Anyone who was interested was welcome to come to see the frescos in his residence. Endangered from 1825 onwards, in 1885, after many trial runs, they were sawn out together with the walls, detached from the masonry behind and re-attached to a wooden framework. In 1887 they were moved from Rome to Berlin where a room was set aside for them on the upper floor of the Nationalgalerie.   *AW*

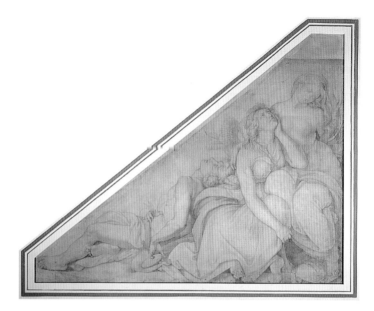

Peter Cornelius (1783–1867)

Midday. Designs for ceiling decorations
in the Göttersaal in the Munich
Glyptothek, 1819
Hyacinthus, Clytie and Leucothea
The Chariot of Apollo
Apollo and Daphne
Charcoal on paper, mounted on canvas
59 x 67 in., 66 ½ x 84 ¾ in., 59 x 67 in.
Acquired 1867

When the Bavarian crown prince visited Rome on his journey to Italy, he
showed a particular interest in the frescos in Jakob Salomon Bartholdy's residence (pp. 40–41) and immediately
took steps to have similar work carried
out in Munich. Julius Schnorr von
Carolsfeld reported on the prince's
plans: "He is concerned as to how he
could be of service to art, so it seems
now to be his firm intention to commission significant works, so-called
works for eternity. Cornelius, whom he
particularly likes, has been asked to decorate, with frescos that is, the three large
rooms in the style of Raphaelesque log-
gias with arabesques and mythological
scenes." In the autumn of 1819 the artist
began his work in Munich and by the

end of the year he had drawn the groups
of figures for 'Midday': the sun god
Apollo on his chariot, three offerings of
love to Apollo on the left-hand side, and
the Daphne myth on the right. After
1820, the designs were carried out on
plaster, partially by other artists. At the
time, originality of design was more
highly valued than the artist's having
personally executed the work. The cycle
of frescos was finished in 1830. During
the Second World War, however, the
frescos were hopelessly destroyed.

Cornelius also accepted a commission
for frescos in the Ludwigskirche (Ludwig Church) in Munich before he followed a summons to Berlin in 1841 and
took the life-size sketches on card with
him. Friedrich Wilhelm IV had commissioned him to decorate the planned
Campo Santo by the cathedral in Berlin
(which in fact was never built). After his
death, these cartoons came as a special
lot to the Nationalgalerie. Within the
context of this intrinsically restrained
art form, these cartoons of mythological
scenes for the Glyptothek are quite
outstanding with their free-flowing,
sensitive lines. They are among Peter
Cornelius's best works and among

the best drawings to come out of nineteenth-century Germany.

"...these drawings speak their own independent technical language which may be compared with that of Dürer, who created it to be written on metal and then reproduced. Likewise, the cartoons by Cornelius are in fact works of art in their own right, and only preparations for other work in the sense that proper drawing is the basis of proper painting." (Max Jordan)   *AW*

Julius Schnorr von Carolsfeld
(1794–1872)

Portrait of Clara Bianca von Quandt,
1820
Oil on wood, 14 ½ x 10 ¼ in.
Acquired 1922

When Johann Gottlob von Quandt, a
wealthy, enthusiastic, influential art
patron, went to Rome on his honey-

moon, he commissioned a portrait of
his wife, Bianca, from his friend Julius
Schnorr. In keeping with Quandt's
wishes, both the composition of the
portrait as well as details of the subject's
clothing and hair go back to the *Portrait
of Joanna of Aragon* (Musée du Louvre,
Paris), at that time attributed to Raphael,
thus quoting one of the most impressive
portraits of the Renaissance and one of

the greatest artists of all time. As well as this ambitious connection, other pictorial elements and the view of the landscape beyond are allusions to Quandt's time in Italy, while the lute is a reference to the music and poetry that Quandt enjoyed with his family during that time.   *BM*

Friedrich Overbeck
(1789–1869)

Portrait of the painter Franz Pforr, 1810/65
Oil on canvas,
24 1/2 x 18 1/2 in.
Acquired 1887

Overbeck painted his idealized portrait of Franz Pforr in Rome in 1810. It is one of the most important Nazarene works and was intended to show his friend in a state of complete happiness. Overbeck created this work in response to a dream of Pforr's, in which the latter saw himself as a history painter in a room lined with old masters, entranced by the presence of a beautiful woman. In Overbeck's painting Pforr, finely dressed in old German costume, sits in the arch of a Gothic window. Like a Madonna, his "wife" is reading in the Bible as she kneels, holding her handwork. The background of an old German town and an Italian coastline evokes the Nazarene ideal of the inseparable bond uniting German and Italian art.   *BV*

Carl Philipp Fohr
(1795–1818)

Knights in front of the Charcoal Burner's Hut, 1816
Oil on canvas, 21 1/4 x 26 in.
Acquired 1931

Shortly before leaving Heidelberg for Rome in 1816,

Fohr painted this work, inspired by Friedrich de la Motte Fouqué's courtly romance, *Der Zauberring*. The poetic quality of the light in this mysterious moonlit scene is quite masterly. The impulse for the work had come from the paintings by old German masters that Fohr had seen in the collection owned by the Boisserée brothers, as well as from the medieval legends and courtly games that the German Romantics had revived.   *BV*

John Constable   (1776–1837)

The Grove, or the Admiral's House,
Hampstead, 1821–22
Oil on canvas, 26 ½ x 19 ¾ in.
Acquired 1905, gift of Paul Freiherr von
Merling

After 1819 Constable, one of the leading English landscape painters of his day,
used to spend the summers in Hampstead. He later moved there altogether.
In Hampstead he produced numerous
landscape and cloud studies that are fascinating for their lively perception of
atmospheric conditions and
for their spontaneous, infinitely subtle painterly technique. The admiral's house
is romantically secluded
among trees and shrubs, and
touched by an uneasy light.
The building itself com-
bines the characteristic
shape of English chimney
stacks with an unusual flat
roof that the admiral had
had put on a few years previously. The house suc-
cumbs to the superior power of nature, as do the small
accessory figures in the
foreground. The force of
the elements, the light, and
even the damp breeze fol-
lowing a passing shower are
palpable. The intensity of
Constable's observation of nature readily
identifies him as a precursor of the
plein-air painters. In this work he goes
beyond the mere depiction of light
effects, bringing to life the movement
and texture of the clouds, the wind, and
the damp air.   *BM*

Carl Blechen   (1798–1840)

Storm in the Roman Campagna, 1829
Oil on cardboard, 10 ⅘ x 17 ½ in.
On loan from the Federal Republic of
Germany

During his sojourn in Italy in 1828/29 Blechen stayed in Rome for several months. From there he would often visit the barren, slightly hilly plain of the Roman Campagna. In numerous oil sketches, usually in an oblong panorama-like format, he captured the spacious breadth of this landscape, paying special attention to the light and cloud phenomena. Behind the greenish brown foreground, the series of arches of a Roman aqueduct extends through the sunlit middle ground. Dominating the landscape is a dome-like gloomy sky, threatening a thunderstorm. *BV*

Carl Blechen (1798–1840)

Forest Path near Spandau,
c. 1834
Oil on canvas, 28 3/4 x 40 in.
Gift of Counsellor of Commerce Glaser in 1890

During his late period, Blechen painted a series of forest and swamp landscapes in which he picked up the mysteriously dark, fantastic natural scenery of his Romantic early work. Surrounded by the impenetrable density of a forest, a young peasant woman carrying a bundle of hay stands on a small wooden bridge.

A storm has left behind numerous puddles and pools of water on the muddy ground. Gloomy branches hang down from massive tall trees; tree trunks against the light bend over a watercourse. The painting's three vanishing points make the forest interior look like the nave and two aisles of a basilica. Only a few individual rays of light penetrate the cathedral-like vault of dense foliage and scatter restlessly among the deep shadows of the forest. Blechen used the tension of contrasts between light and dark to give this picturesque scene dramatic highlights. As the central focus of the light, the sunlit figure of the woman corresponds to the bright window formed by a clearing that affords a view of a Gothic church surrounded by water. *BV*

As one of the most famous sights in the region around Rome, the Villa d'Este attracted many artists. Blechen was fascinated by the sixteenth-century building, the park with its pools and fountains, and not least by the cypress trees. Here the house and its grounds are depicted as monumental and dramatic. The light falls sideways, softly and hazily, with a substance all its own. Figures walk in the avenue wearing Spanish court dress or cardinal's purple. Like a kind of arabesque, they loosen the strictly axial nature of the composition and convey the mannerist spirit of the scene. _BV_

Carl Blechen (1798–1840)

The Park of the Villa d'Este,
c. 1832
Oil on canvas, 50 1/4 x 37 in.
From the Berliner Stadtschloß

Carl Blechen (1798–1840)

The Interior of the Palm House,
1832
Oil on paper on canvas, 25 1/4 x 22 in.
Acquired 1891, from the Brose Collection

In 1832 Friedrich Wilhelm III commissioned Blechen to paint the palm house that had been constructed to Schinkel's designs on the Pfaueninsel (Peacock Island). The plan was to make a diptych for the king to give to his daughter, the tsarina of Russia. Blechen made careful preparations for this commission which meant a lot to him. In addition to numerous drawings he made this outstanding study, the sun flooding into the space with its tropical plants and fragrant climate. Waiting odalisques heighten the sense of oriental magic already conjured up by the Indian feel of the architecture. _BV_

Carl Blechen   (1798–1840)

Gorge near Amalfi, 1831
Oil on canvas, 43 1/2 x 30 1/2 in.
Acquired 1882

In 1828 Blechen travelled to Italy where the southern landscape with its particular colours and light inspired him to a whole number of paintings. He rode through the valley near Amalfi on a donkey, tirelessly sketching and drawing. Two years later, after his return to Ber-

lin, he painted this mountain landscape. Bright light pours into the valley. A group of woodcutters are felling trees for the paper mill, seen with smoke ascending from its chimney. By the strength of the verticals in this picture and the striking contrasts of light and dark, Blechen lends a dramatic air to this extremely picturesque piece.   *BV*

Carl Blechen (1798–1840)

The Neustadt-Eberswalde Rolling Mill,
c. 1830
Oil on wood, 10 x 13 in.
Acquired 1891 from the Brose Collection

In Eberswalde Blechen saw the brassworks on the Finow Canal, one of the
first metalworking factories in the Mark
Brandenburg. Impressed by the sheer
size of the works, he made several drawings on the spot, which served as the
basis for this painting. What appears as
prosaic industrial reality in the sketches
is ennobled in the oil painting and at the
same time distanced by the figures in the
foreground. An angler sits thoughtfully
on the banks of the Finow Canal, while
two other fishermen are pulling in their
nets: an idyll very much in the tradition
of the seventeenth and the eighteenth
centuries, while the rolling mill rises up
threateningly in the background like a
mighty fort.

Heavy, almost leaden smoke pours
out of the chimney stacks into the clear,
yellowish evening sky, casting a greenish-
black shadow on the water. This work
counts as one of the earliest European
depictions of industrial sites, along with
Christian Koester's 1810 *Stauf Copper-
wire Works with Neu-Leinigen* and Alfred
Rethel's 1834 *Harkort Factory.*   BV

Carl Blechen (1798–1840)

View of Roofs and Gardens,
c. 1835
Oil on canvas, 7 3/4 x 10 1/4 in.
Acquired 1891, from the Brose Collection

The view is from Blechen's flat at
9 Kochstraße in Berlin. Abandoning the
traditional schemata of landscape painting, Blechen risked an unusual composition that seems more like a detail from
a larger work. On the right is the corner
of the roof of the house, while on the
left is an open view of the backyard and
the adjoining garden. It has
just rained and there are
puddles in the yard. The
roof reflects the gentle
light. The subtly gradated
colours create a muted
atmosphere. For this work
Blechen chose an utterly
unspectacular motif from
everyday life, simply painting what he saw, spontane-
ously and expressively — a
daring move later taken up
and further developed by
Adolph Menzel.   BV

Carl Rottmann   (1797–1850)

The Battlefield at Marathon, 1849
Oil on canvas, 35³/₄ x 35¹/₂ in.
Acquired 1875

This visionary portrayal of a battle was one of Rottmann's last works. It reproduces — although more succinctly and with greater symbolism — the *Marathon* fresco of 1848 (encaustic on stone, Neue Pinakothek, Munich). However, this work does not in any sense depict the historical event of the Battle of Marathon in 490 B.C. when the Greeks decisively defeated the Persians: it has become a battle between the elements, a struggle between light and darkness.

Rottmann had already transposed the events onto a cosmic level in his studies, a charcoal sketch on card and a watercolour study from 1841, and the fresco also shows the battle as an elemental struggle. In the 1820s Germany had been swept by enthusiasm for Greek resistance to Turkish rule, which struck a chord in the German consciousness of the time. In 1832 Prince Otto of Bavaria was declared King of Greece and a series of frescos on Greek history was planned for the arcades in the Hofgarten in Munich. In 1834–35 Rottmann, in order to research this work, travelled to Greece, then impoverished despite its proud past. Just as that journey perhaps destroyed Rottmann's vision of Greece, so the failed 1848 revolution destroyed the German dream of a just state. As a review from 1849 in the *Kunstblatt* shows, Rottmann's contemporaries already saw this glowering "Marathon" picture by the ageing artist as a "political landscape."   *AW*

talking at the entrance to a shop. A coach is turning into the street from Klosterstraße with Berlin's oldest church, St. Nicholas, rising up in the background.   *BV*

Eduard Gaertner   (1801–1877)

Rear view of the Houses at Schloßfreiheit, 1855
Oil on canvas, 22 x 37³/₄ in.
Property of the Verein der Freunde der Nationalgalerie

Gaertner's painting shows the area of middle-class Berlin that had to give way, during the Wilhelmine era, to the grand public face that the emperor and his family wanted to present. In 1896 the whole row of houses of the Schloßfreiheit on the banks of the Spree close to the palace was demolished and replaced with the Monument to Emperor. The name Schloßfreiheit came into being in 1678 when the Magistrate of Friedrichswerder was denied ultimate judicial control of this area. The fine bourgeois facades with their warehouses and gold and silver shops are overshadowed by the dome of the palace. On the opposite bank there are coaches, people out for a stroll, and children playing. The whole scene is framed by important works by Schinkel: on the right the Building Academy and on the left the bridge to the palace.   *BV*

Eduard Gaertner   (1801–1877)

Parochialstraße, 1831
Oil on canvas, 15¹/₄ x 11¹/₂ in.
Acquired 1861, Consul Wagener bequest

Parochialstraße was typical of the areas of Berlin where craftsmen and tradesmen both worked and lived. Gaertner has captured the atmosphere of a typical workday with a clear affection for detail. The early morning sun touches the top floors of the narrow houses. The cobbled street is already bustling with activity: to the left a pipe-smoking coppersmith with his wares on display and, across the street, an inn and women

Johann Erdmann Hummel
(1769–1852)

The Granite Dish in the Berlin Lust-
garten, 1831
Oil on canvas, 26 x 35 in.
Acquired 1905

There are two levels of meaning to the
painting of the granite dish as seen in
1831 on a slightly raised podium in the
Lustgarten. At first sight Hummel — a
Biedermeier painter who was often
known as "Perspective Hummel" — is
simply chronicling the temporary erec-
tion of the massively heavy, highly pol-
ished dish from the factory of the industrialist Cantian, thereby proudly
depicting an outstanding technical
achievement of his day. And yet at the
same time Hummel is parodying the age
of the Industrial Revolution he admired
so much, showing Cantian representing
industry and an uhlan caval-
ryman representing the state
— small and distorted, up-
side down on the underside
of the dish — while the rest
of the populace of Berlin are
literally standing on their
heads, from petit-bourgeois
to grand lady in a poke
bonnet. *BM*

Carl Begas the Elder   (1797–1854)

The Artist's Parents, after 1826
Oil on canvas, 16 x 32 in.
Acquired 1906, gift of Building Officer
M. Friedeberg

Begas was the father of four sons, all of
whom painted or sculpted, and in this
double portrait, painted after his studies
in Paris and Rome, he found a mode of
expression of his own that was both Romantic and Realistic. With an attention
to detail that is reminiscent of Holbein,
he painted his parents in strict profile,
which lends a degree of psychological
authenticity to the two heads against the
dark background. The grotesques on the
frame add an element of symbolism to
the work: while a female figure holds
laurel leaves out to the artist's civil servant
father, a second figure is crowning his
mother with a wreath.   *AW*

Franz Krüger (1797–1857)

Prince Wilhelm Riding Out in
the Company of the Artist, 1836
Oil on canvas, 12 1/4 x 9 1/2 in.
Acquired 1897

As painter to the royal court, Franz
Krüger was often invited to go out riding with Crown Prince Wilhelm, who
was later to become emperor. In this
small scale work showing the two riding
together, Krüger depicts the Prince and
himself as private individuals without
any of the trappings of courtly grandeur.
Since a storm is brewing, they are trot-
ting quickly back home. The heir to the
throne is distinguished from his companion by his clothes, a nobler horse,
more elegant posture and foreground
position. The artist is seen behind him
in profile, upright and concentrating,
sending a sharply observant sideways
glance to the prince. The latter's spirited
horse seems to be moving so quickly
that it is almost floating, while the way
the prince apparently just happens to be
looking back at his dog creates the cru-
cial diagonal lines that mark him out as
the center of this invigorating, brightly
illuminated scene. *BV*

Franz Krüger (1797–1857)

Parade on the Opernplatz in Berlin,
1824–30
Oil on canvas, 98 x 147 1/4 in.
Acquired 1928

Krüger's glittering masterpiece was
commissioned in 1824 by the Russian
Grand Duke Nicholas, the son-in-law
of the King of Prussia. It was taken to
the Winter Palace in St. Petersburg.
Shortly before the First World War, the
picture returned to Berlin as a present
from the tsar to the emperor and was
stored in the Stadtschloß (City Palace).
It was not until 1928 that it was acquired
by the Nationalgalerie. Krüger depicted
a panoramic view of the Prussian "via
triumphalis" with total topographic
accuracy, showing a parade of the sixth
Brandenburg Kürassierregiment (dra-
goons) led by the grand duke, later to be

Tsar Nicholas I. He is seen at the head of his troops riding towards King Friedrich Wilhelm III, who salutes in his plumed hat, positioned on horseback opposite the Neue Wache (surveillance building). Contrary to the conventions governing the composition of works depicting historical events, the painter has positioned the monarch on the very edge of the scene. Neither the princely protagonists nor the parade itself are at the center of attention. Instead it is the representatives of bourgeois Berlin who occupy the pavement area in the foreground in front of a group of chestnut trees between the Zeughaus (arsenal) and Schinkel's Neue Wache, as if showing themselves off on an open-air stage. Here there is a general crowding of the "best known figures in Berlin with no distinction as to class: professors, artists, civil servants, actresses, actors, statesmen, military personnel, the daily visitors to the coffee houses and public promenades, the best known gawpers." (Athansius Raczýnski, *Geschichte der neueren deutschen Kunst*, Vol. 3, 1841) Krüger has faithfully captured many of his contemporaries with evident sympathy, including such personalities as the sculptors Schadow and Rauch, the master builder Schinkel, the singer Henriette Sontag and the violinist Paganini. But there is a place for the ordinary folk too, with the artist devoting particular care to the cobbler's boy. Krüger avoided any hint of stiffness and uniformity. He was much more concerned to represent the multiplicity and vitality of the social and intellectual life of Berlin. *BV*

Alfred Rethel   (1816–1859)

Portrait of the Artist's Mother,
1833–35
Oil on canvas, 24 x 18 1/2 in.
Acquired 1935

This early work by Rethel, renowned as
the creator of the Aachen Frescos, was
to become a bench mark of German
portraiture in the nineteenth century.
Painted when Rethel was a student
under Wilhelm von Schadow at the
Düsseldorf Academy, its style clearly
shows the influence of the Nazarenes.
The quality of the portrait is evident
in the minute observation of detail
that brings the subject so close to the
viewer.   *KS*

Johann Peter Hasenclever
(1810–1853)

The Reading Room,
1843
Oil on canvas, 28 x 39 1/2 in.
Acquired 1861,
Consul Wagener bequest

Since the early nineteenth
century, public reading
rooms had been important
meeting places for conversation and the spread of
enlightened thinking. In its
content, *The Reading Room*
follows on after other works
by Hasenclever: *The Politi-
cians* (1833–34), *The Newspaper Readers* (1835) and
The Politician (1839). In all
of these an important role
is played by the press as a
means of forming public
opinion. In Germany in
1842, censorship grew and
1843 saw the banning in
Düsseldorf of the news-
paper *Die Rheinische
Zeitung*, which had been
edited by a friend of
Hasenclever's, the poet
Ferdinand Freiligrath.   *AW*

Carl Spitzweg   (1808–1885)

The Poor Poet, 1839
Oil on canvas, 14 1/4 x 17 1/2 in.
Acquired 1908, stolen 1989

Spitzweg himself regarded this work as his first successful genre painting, and it was to become his most famous. In a poor, unheated attic room, a poet sits up in bed, wrapped in a coat and a blanket. Although the sun is shining in through the window, the snow-covered roofs opposite show that it is a cold winter's day. With his quill in his mouth, the poet is certainly not thinking about his poetry: instead his entire attention is taken up by the flea that he has just caught between his fingers. His manuscripts are lying in front of the stove and will shortly go up in smoke.

Spitzweg's subtle humor was aimed at the then inviolable ideal of the artist or the poet *per se*. He dared to criticize the rather literary style of the Nazarenes, which provoked a variety of responses, including even outright rejection. *BV*

Carl Spitzweg (1808–1885)

Flying Kites, c. 1880–85
Oil on card, 15 x 4³/₄ in.
Acquired 1908

This painting, flooded with light, is a late work by Spitzweg. It depicts kite-flying, an activity that delights adults and children alike. Spitzweg chose the Theresienwiese on the edge of Munich as the setting for this scene, and the silhouette of the town can be seen disappearing in the background. By means of an unusually tall, narrow format, Spitzweg lends a sense of infinitude to the sky, awakening in the viewer an involuntary longing to share the kite's lightness. *BV*

Moritz von Schwind   (1804–1871)

Farewell at Dawn, 1859
Oil on card, 14 ¼ x 9 ½ in.
Acquired 1910

In works — both poetic and accessible — which the artist himself referred to as "occasional poems," Schwind liked to record episodes from his own life. He also described this series of small idylls

as "Travel Pictures." Scenes, like this one of his departure from Vienna thirty years before, are concentrated into a lyrical image. Here, the painting achieves its timeless relevance by the telling way it captures that decisive moment of the traveller looking back and forwards at the same time.   *AW*

Ludwig Richter   (1803–1884)

The Well in the Wood at Ariccia, 1831
Oil on canvas, 18 ½ x 24 in.
Acquired 1914, bequest from G.A. Freund

Both idealizing and longing for the land where he had become an artist, Ludwig Richter constantly drew on his memories of Italy during his time as a drawing teacher in Meißen. The poetic content of his works takes up important issues of the time: walking and resting, distance and closeness, which in Richter's late Romantic painting was soon to assume a particularly intimate form.   *AW*

Moritz von Schwind   (1804–1871)

The Rose, or the Artists' Journey, 1846–47
Oil on canvas, 85 x 52 ¾ in.
Acquired 1874

Like many of Schwind's other "picture novellas," *The Rose* tells the story of a romanticized Middle Ages, of German woods and birdsong and of unfulfilled dreams of love. "The hero," wrote the painter, "is the last musician, a man with lofty ideas" and yet "a ruined genius." The viewer can guess what longing will be awakened by the dropped rose. Disillusion was a central theme in Schwind's work.   *CK*

Ludwig Richter (1803–1884)

Lake in the Riesengebirge, 1839
Oil on canvas, 24 3/4 x 34 3/4 in.
Acquired 1878

In 1836 pictures from the modern
Düsseldorf school of painting were
exhibited for the first time in Dresden.
Ludwig Richter was impressed above all
by realistic nature studies by August
Schirmer. They had "opened my eyes to
a way of observing and understanding
nature, for which I am intensely grate-
ful." An echo of this reaction still lingers
in this dramatic landscape rendered in,
for Richter, an unusually painterly style.

AW

Johan Christian Dahl
(1788–1857)

Stormclouds over the Castle Tower in
Dresden, c. 1825
Oil on card, 8 1/4 x 8 3/4 in.
Acquired 1911, gift from Ludwig Justi

Following his journey to Italy in
1820–21, during which he developed a
spontaneous, sketchlike style of painting, Dahl carried out a series of cloud
studies in Dresden. It seems likely that
his friend Carus had given him the idea
to paint this motif, on the basis of Luke
Howard's cloud theories. In this study
with its uncommonly sure, free brushwork, Dahl captured the threatening
build-up of clouds above the castle
tower. A few touches of paint were all
he needed to show the tower catching
the light of the sun as it breaks through
the clouds. The seething drama of the
stormclouds serves as a Romantic symbol of the power of nature at the same
time as being a perfectly neutral observation of meteorological phenomena.
With these small studies of daringly
selected details Dahl was treading a
path that was already showing the
way towards the principles of plein-air
painting. *AW*

Wilhelm von Kobell   (1766–1853)

Riders at the Tegernsee, 1832
Oil on oak panel, 11 x 10¼ in.
Acquired 1928

These works by Kobell, in a style that
he developed after 1815, were known
as "Scenes of Encounters" — pictures
where figures meet and yet remain
silently isolated from one another. *The
Riders at the Tegernsee* encounter each
other in the bright central area of the
picture, at a crossroads as though on a
stage or a plinth. A dark chain of mountains provides the backdrop to the scene,
and the wall of rain is not disturbing but
rather heightens the sense of symmetry
and concentration. The protagonists —
a distinguished-looking rider on a grey
horse standing parallel to the picture
plane, a groom to the left and a farm

horse to the right — are all clearly
delineated and at no point do they over-
lap each other. This style of representation could be described as a "layered
relief composition" (Wichmann). In its
expression it is naive yet surreal. The
figures are laid out as in a child's picture
or in a show-box. We see a scene where
the moment of encounter is prolonged
into infinity by the frozen participants;
something everyday and perfectly mundane becomes a kind of ritual, which is
matched both by the cool, light tones of
the picture and its glazed finish; even
the long shadows are light.   *AW*

Ferdinand Georg Waldmüller
(1793–1865)

Portrait of the Mother of Captain
von Stierle-Holzmeister, c. 1819
Oil on canvas, 21¼ x 16¼ in.
Acquired 1909

At the age of twenty-six, Waldmüller
received his first important portrait
commission from Captain Joseph von
Stierle-Holzmeister who asked him to
paint a true-to-life portrait of his
mother, formerly an actress at the Hof-

burg, later to become privy
councilor Mierck. In a
domestic setting, in a red
house dress, facing forwards
and completely filling the
picture frame, the old lady
comes extremely close to
the viewer. The colour,
light, and shade of both her
skin and her clothes are
portrayed with a high
degree of refinement. No
detail has been ignored,
nothing has been prettified.
There is no sign of any
neck, just her heavy head
resting on her shoulders. To
meet the terms of the commission, Waldmüller aban-
doned the traditions of
actors' portraits as he was
later often to do. The
intention was to convey the
sitter's individuality, not
status. In his portraits, Waldmüller united
natural, living reality with sensually
pleasing painting.   *KS*

Ferdinand Georg Waldmüller
(1793–1865)

On All Souls' Day, 1839
Oil on wood, 14¾ x 18¾ in.
From the Figdor Collection

The small scale of this work lends it the
character of a devotional picture. Two

women, presumably moth-
er and daughter, kneel in a
cemetery in front of a grave
decorated with fresh flowers. The monumental forms
of the women dressed in
mourning stand out like silhouettes against the cloudy
background. The light falls
on their faces. Waldmüller
was later to virtually repeat
this composition with its
echoes of English genre
painting in his *Devotion of
St. John* of 1840 (in private
ownership).   *KS*

Ferdinand Georg Waldmüller (1793–1865)

Prater Landscape, 1830
(Along the Riverbank, Elms by the Water)
Oil on panel, 28 x 36 in.
Acquired 1905 from the art dealer H.O. Miethke in Vienna; lost from 1945 to 1999; returned in 2000

Compared to his portraits and genre scenes, Waldmüller's landscapes are fewer in number but not less in importance. They demonstrate that plein air painting can even be consistent by doing without an emphatically subjective, spontaneous brushstroke, thus allowing the depiction of minute detail. The harsh light and the abrupt spatial contrasts of Waldmüller's later paintings are not yet to be found in this early Prater landscape. Spreading out peacefully under the bushy foliage of the elms, the green of the meadow continues into the bright distance. The horizon is remarkably low, delineated by the new blocks of flats in Vienna's Leopoldstadt. For stylistic reasons the very small, partly obscured signature has usually been read as "1830." That would make this picture the first in a series of about ten small and four larger landscapes showing Vienna's Prater. The last one of these, the so-called *Large Prater Landscape* (1849, Vienna, Österreichische Galerie im Belvedere) clearly seems to have more weight and pathos than the Berlin picture, which is bathed in cool morning light and populated by only one small accessory figure. CK

Besides painting landscapes, in his later years Waldmüller became increasingly interested in portraying everyday life in the country, often combining harmonious tranquillity with an element of social criticism. As his models he took the children running about in the lanes, peasants and serving girls. In his later genre paintings, he focused in particular on portraying large groups of animated figures. Drenched in bright sunlight, different groups of fair-goers happen to meet each other. Triangular groups and touches of blue link the composition into a whole. The lines of the houses accentuate the underlying structure, with the tree rising up in the background constituting the only fixed vertical. This way of handling lighting and groups of people bears witness to Waldmüller's awareness of stagecraft: from 1811 until 1813 he was employed as a designer in the theater at Agram (Zagreb). KS

Ferdinand Georg Waldmüller (1793–1865)

Return from the Church Fair, c. 1859–60
Oil on wood, 29 1/4 x 37 1/4 in.
Acquired 1897, sold in 1935 to the State Chancery; bought back in 1991 with the assistance of the Ernst von Siemens-Kulturfond

linear structure of his works and their meticulous, naively-honest painterly portrayal of detail is immediately evocative of the works of the old masters in Germany. The portrait of Frau von Zallinger (1806–1890) is one of his most challenging works. The young woman regards the viewer calmly and searchingly. Neither the clarity of the light nor the painting's harmonious tones dispel the sense of coolly realistic objectivity. Wasmann's portraits pay allegiance to that greater form where colour and line become one, thus following a path that Leibl was later to pursue to its ultimate heights. *KS*

Friedrich Wasmann (1805–1886)

Portrait of Frau Josepha von Zallinger, née Amplatz, 1842
Oil on canvas, 21 3/4 x 18 in.
Acquired 1932

A native of Hamburg, Wasmann moved to Tirol after his studies in Dresden and Munich, where he worked painting portraits for the nobility and the bourgeoisie alike. His style as a portrait artist was rooted in Romantic-Nazarene attitudes, while at the same time the clear,

Louis Ferdinand von Rayski (1806–1890)

Portrait of Christine Freifrau von Schönberg, c. 1864–68
Oil on canvas, 36 1/4 x 30 3/4 in.
Acquired 1915

Christine von Schönberg (1838–1903) was the second wife of a close friend of Rayski's, the Saxon Count Erich von Schönberg. Contrasting with the velvety black of her clothes, the sitter's rosy cheeks and brown hair stand out against

the diffuse darkness of the background. Rayski has captured the image on canvas with verve and a generous brush. The deep sense of calm flowing from the young woman contrasts with the sketchy style of the painting. Positioned solidly upright and defining the central axis of the painting, the sitter both occupies the space and is locked into her own world as it were. This work shows Rayski the portraitist at his most succinct, reminiscent of eighteenth-century portraitists and yet at the same time close to the French Impressionists. *KS*

Louis Ferdinand von Rayski
(1806–1890)

Portrait of Count Haubold von Einsiedel, 1855
Oil on canvas, 28 ³/₄ x 24 ¹/₂ in.
Acquired 1906

The nobility in nineteenth-century Saxony was well served by the portraitist Ferdinand von Rayski. Three generations of the Einsiedel family had their portraits painted by him at their home, Schloß Milke, in Saxony. This was where Rayski also painted the portrait of the young Count Haubold (1844–1868) who was to die in early manhood. No emblems of his status indicate the sitter's social rank. His dress is plain and formal, yet somehow careless. The seated pose, which is only hinted at, is relaxed as befits the portrait of an eleven-year-old. Nevertheless the choice of a half-length portrait showing the boy's self-confident posture with slightly bent arms does evoke formal Baroque portraiture. Strict attention to the axes of the composition and the monumental way the space is filled define the overall structure as in the portrait of Christine von Schönberg. The use of colour fields sets it apart from the precision painting of the Biedermeier period, and the muted, earthy, almost monochrome tonality is reminiscent of Courbet's palette.

KS

Adolph Menzel   (1815–1905)

The Berlin-Potsdam Railway, 1847
Oil on canvas, 16 1/2 x 20 1/2 in.
Acquired 1899

The Potsdam railway line was opened
after five years' work in 1838, that is to
say during the pioneering years of this
new means of transport, which fur-
nished Menzel throughout his life with
subjects for his paintings and drawings.
As may be seen from an earlier drawing
of 1845, at first Menzel was only interested in the sharp curve of the tracks
through the countryside which was

disturbed by the arrival of transport
technology. In the painted version, he
added the locomotive with its string of
cars, filling the air with grey smoke. CK

Adolph Menzel   (1815–1905)

Building Site with Willows, 1846
Oil on canvas, 16 1/4 x 21 3/4 in.
Acquired 1906

There is almost something threatening
in the profusion of wind-tossed, silvery,
shimmering branches in the foreground
of this picture. Menzel discovered these

willows not far from his flat
in the Berlin in Schöne-
berger Straße near what was
later to become the Land-
wehr Canal. Under a blue
sky and bathed in harsh
sunlight, beyond the timeless sight of horses drinking,
as yet unfinished red and
yellow brick houses with
bricklayers working on
the scaffolding herald the
advance of the city into the
countryside.   CK

Adolph Menzel (1815–1905)

The Balcony Room, 1845
Oil on card, 22 $^3/_4$ x 18 $^1/_2$ in.
Acquired 1903

Of all the examples of the painterly spontaneity of the young Menzel's art, *The Balcony Room* is one of the earliest and also most admired. Unlike contemporary Biedermeier interior views, this painting gives no conclusive information as to the room's aspect. Two thirds of the surfaces are simply empty. It is only in the mirror that there is any detail: a petit-bourgeois inventory of the most mundane sort, oddly disarranged and far from homey. Large areas of the picture are "unfinished," which in fact means that the paint, not depicting something else, retains a life of its own. The actual theme of the painting is immaterial: strong light pours into the room with a gust of wind that blows the fine, white curtains inwards, and that is all the viewer discovers about the otherwise undefined outside world. A lack of consistency in observing precise perspectives, following the rules of linear construction, makes the floor appear to incline towards the viewer. This suggests different stages of perception simultaneously.

CK

Adolph Menzel (1815–1905)

The Théâtre du Gymnase, 1856
Oil on canvas, 18 x 24 ½ in.
Acquired 1906

Menzel was often compared to his
French contemporaries, usually in the
search for a German counterpart to the
French Impressionists, even perhaps for
a precursor. However one-sided this
view may have been, his *Théâtre du
Gymnase* cannot be dissociated from
thoughts of theater scenes by Daumier
and, above all, Degas, although the

latter did not even exist
when Menzel painted this
work. Menzel had visited
Paris for the first time one
year previously and ever
after called it "Babel." The
notion of an excited but
anonymous audience in the
confusing artificial light
leaves less opportunity for
narrative detail than in
Menzel's later scenes of
town life. But already in
this work, there is no clear
central focus of attention: from the
actors playing a musical comedy in
contemporary dress to the stalls and the
boxes, everything seems to be periph-
eral. The transience of the motifs is in
no way commensurate with the drama
of the colour combination — reminiscent of Delacroix — of blue, red, and
golden-yellow.   *CK*

Adolph Menzel (1815–1905)

Studio Wall, 1852
Oil on paper bonded to wood,
        24 x 17 ¼ in.
        Acquired 1906

Once in 1852, and again in
1872, Menzel depicted the
red-painted wall of his studio with plaster casts hanging on it. In both pictures
light comes from below,
apparently breathing dis-
turbing life into the objects.
In the second, larger version
(Hamburg Kunsthalle), the
death masks dominate while
in the earlier version it is the
casts of limbs, and although
these are taken from live
models, their fragmentation
and proximity to a skull and
a skinned hand make them
seem more like parts from a
corpse. Menzel has con-
sciously excluded those classical casts that are part of the
study program in any art
academy: the palette at the

lower edge of the picture reads much like a signature below an allegorical declaration of allegiance to the study of nature itself. *CK*

Adolph Menzel (1815–1905)

The Artist's Bedroom in Ritterstraße, 1847
Oil on card, 22 x 18 in.
Acquired 1905

Two years after *The Balcony Room*, Menzel used the same format apparently to combine two favorite motifs of the time: the interior view and the view from a window. In this work, the two both balance and compete with each other. Contrary to expectation, the viewer's gaze is hurried past the foreground with its large forms, broad brushstrokes, and marked perspectives to the scene in the distance with its backyard and houses, which are more detailed, sharper, and more colorful than the foreground. The shapeless mass of the bed, that seems to heave ponderously under the thin folds of the coverlet, takes up almost the entire lower half of the picture. The distant idyll of everyday life is cut off from the viewer by a distinctly hostile zone. *CK*

Adolph Menzel (1815–1905)

Flute Concert with Frederick the Great
in Sanssouci, 1850–52
Oil on canvas, 56 x 80¾ in.
Acquired 1875

In the 1840s Menzel produced numerous illustrations for Franz Kugler's ever
popular *History of Frederick the Great*.
Menzel's intense work on the times and
character of Friedrich II, who reigned
from 1740 to 1786, was to bear fruit,
even apart from the book illustrations
which made Menzel famous. Along
with the self-contained "society piece,"
Die Tafelrunde, the *Flute Concert* may be
regarded as one of the paintings where
Menzel, in free and full possession of his
powers as a painter, deepened and trans-
formed his subjects in a subtly shifting
mix of world history and parochial
patriotism. The King of Prussia, a pas-
sionately keen flautist who also composed for the flute, is playing on the
occasion of a visit from his sister, the
Margravine of Bayreuth. Keeping time
with his left foot, he is improvising at a
high music stand which prevents any eye
contact with the ensemble, so that the
composition, arranged parallel to the
picture plane, is divided by his figure
into audience on the left and chamber
ensemble on the right. Among the pronounced verticals of the composition,
the extreme foreshortening of the flute
is very noticeable. Menzel's portrayal of
the scene, with its attention to historical
accuracy in both dress and furnishings,
does not depict the instrument as simply
another anecdotal detail, but rather concentrates on the musically flickering,
warm candlelight of the theatrically
illuminated concert room in Sanssouci,
which seems to flow backwards with its
own choreographed rhythm. Rather
than an apotheosis of the cultivation of
the arts at the court of Frederick the
Great, Menzel has created an atmospheric portrayal of music-making. *BM*

Adolph Menzel (1815–1905)

"Bonsoir, messieurs!" Frederick II in the
Castle at Lissa, Sketch, 1856
Oil on paper on canvas, 12¾ x 10 in.
Acquired 1889

In his *History of Frederick the Great*, Franz
Kugler describes a fictive story during
the Seven Years' War: after the victory
at the Battle of Leuthen, the king took
a troop of men and followed the enemy
to where they had fled. When the Prus-
sians came under fire, the king called for
reinforcements. However, he himself
rode on to the Castle at Lissa, where he

greeted the surprised enemy officers with the words:"Bonsoir, messieurs! No doubt you were not expecting me. But might one find a lodging here for the night?" In their confusion, the Austrians did not notice that the king was as yet without his men, who only arrived later to capture the enemy in the castle. Menzel situates the recognition scene in the stairwell at the moment when Frederick II is boldly entering the castle. The consternation and horror felt by the Austrians match the Prussian king's audacity. In 1858 Menzel created a large-scale version (Hamburg Kunsthalle) of this sketch. *BV*

Adolph Menzel (1815–1905)

Frederick the Great and his Marshals before the Battle of Leuthen, 1859–61
Oil on canvas, 125 ¼ x 167 in.
Acquired 1905

A group of generals is gathered round Frederick II. Following the defeats that Prussia had already suffered in the Seven Years' War, the king was giving his generals the option of withdrawing from service before the impending, decisive conflict. Indeed, the Battle of Leuthen in 1757, which restored large parts of Silesia to Prussian rule, was to be a turning point in the history of Prussia. Menzel never completed this, his most representative painting of Frederick II, and even scratched certain parts out again. Yet the subtle, earthy-misty tones of the winter's morning and the grey-brown of the officers' coats with sparse touches of red, hold the picture together despite its fragmented condition. The painting affords some insight into Menzel's working practices: while some figures exist only as outlines, others are already completely finished. *BM*

Adolph Menzel (1815–1905)

The Iron Rolling Mill (Modern Cyclopes), 1872–75
Oil on canvas, 62 ¼ x 100 in.
Acquired 1875

The theme of physical labor had already made its entry into the pictorial world of the nineteenth century with Gustave Courbet's *Stonebreakers* of 1851. Menzel made his first drawings of an industrial setting, the Heckmann Brassworks in Berlin, in 1869. The impulse for *The Iron Rolling Mill* most probably came from Menzel's friend Paul Meyerheim, who was working on a series on the history of the railways for the industrialist Albert Borsig.

In 1872 Menzel travelled to Königs-hütte in Upper Silesia in order to famili-arize himself with factory conditions there, and spent weeks making hun-dreds of preparatory sketches. Drawing

on the creative powers he had gained from his rich experience of painting large group scenes, here Menzel creates a composition positively filled with fig-ures demonstrating the force of modern industrial work. In the steam-filled gloom, flickering lights and bizarre shadows merge to become a demonic drama depicting the struggle between men and machines. The animated, tonally dynamic central section of the picture is set against the calmer upper third of the composition with its diffuse daylight. The apparent chaos of the complicated iron rolling equipment emphasizes the dependence of the workers, who must submit to the un-bending workings of the machinery.

Yet Menzel's main concern was not the socially critical aspect of this scene, but the artistic challenge of portraying the production process and the groups of people involved in it. He was inter-

Adolph Menzel (1815–1905)

The Dinner at the Ball, 1878
Oil on canvas, 28 x 35 ½ in.
Acquired 1906

After the 1860s, Menzel was a regular guest at the large gatherings in the Berlin Stadtschloß (City Palace). He recorded his impressions as paintings, of which *The Dinner at the Ball* is the most complex. The company is shown from a high viewpoint during a pause in the dancing. In a vibrant play of colour, Menzel captures small, individual incidents in the midst of *Gründerzeit* (c. 1871–1890) pomp, showing with subtle irony the difficulty of maintaining the correct posture while eating, the chattering of voices, and the overall sense of animation. The throng seems to be without a focal point, but the composition is held together by the movement of the entire crowd towards the viewer. There is no place for detail in this work that is, while sketchy, more of an atmospheric whole. As in earlier interiors, the room is divided and layered by the refraction of the lights at numerous points in the mirrors and chandeliers. The interiors, chandelier light, and magnificent clothes of Menzel's late work balance his contemporaneous street and factory scenes like *The Iron Rolling Mill* and mark his increasing interest in painting large crowds of people. As so often elsewhere, what looks like meticulous attention to detail on Menzel's part turns out to be illusory: neither are the rooms accurately portrayed nor are there any actual portraits of particular individuals in the crowd. The painting conveys a picture of Wilhelmine society whose lustre Menzel was brilliantly able to convey, and yet whose ambivalence he did no more than register as an apparently neutral chronicler. *KS*

ested in everyday life, not in representing the existential threat to humanity posed by the age of the machine. In *The Iron Rolling Mill*, Menzel's artistic skills have reached their greatest heights. *KS*

Reinhold Begas (1831–1911)

Amor and Psyche, 1854–57
Marble, 38 1/4 x 48 3/4 x 30 3/4 in.
Acquired 1971

The story of the love of Amor and Psyche, as related by Apuleius in ancient times, inspired artists into ever new images: Psyche, visited each night by her lover Amor, who nevertheless refuses to reveal his shape and his name, succumbs to curiosity and approaches the sleeping Amor in order to see his true form by the light of an oil lamp. Inadvertently, a drop of oil to falls onto Amor, who flees in shock. Only after Psyche has passed various tests and the gods give their permission, may she marry her lover in the gods' heaven. For his first, large, independent sculpture, Begas chose the dramatic highpoint of the story, when Psyche bends over her lover. The composition is in the traditions of classical sculpture and is structured within a broad-based triangle with Psyche's head marking its highest point. The work is built up on a harmonious oval plinth. The treatment of surfaces and individual shapes alike shows Begas' move from strict linearity to the soft, painterly modelling that was soon to become characteristic of neo-Baroque art. *BM*

Reinhold Begas
(1831–1911)

Pan Comforting Psyche,
1857–58
Marble, 52 x 39 3/4 x 26 1/4 in.
Acquired 1934

Deserted by Amor, her lover, Psyche bemoans her curiosity and its consequences. Agitated yet demure, she is comforted by Pan, the otherwise frivolous god of nature. The subject allowed Begas to unite a range of contrasts within one sculpture: female/male, tender/rough, youthful/old. *BM*

Reinhold Begas
(1831–1911)

Mercury Abducting Psyche,
1870–78
Marble,
80 3/4 x 51 1/4 x 37 1/2 in.
Acquired 1878

The muscular Mercury, the messenger of the gods, takes Psyche to her lover Amor. In this upwards-rising, dramatically spatial sculpture, respectful-devotional love has given way to a coquettish, almost socially acceptable complaisance that was already hinted at in *Pan Comforting Psyche*. The general move, during the *Gründerzeit* (c. 1870–1890), from the classical serenity of content and form towards the neo-Baroque, is characteristic of the developments in sculptural style that Begas did much to define. While his earlier work harmoniously expresses what the figures have in common, this work is much closer to Baroque outbursts of emotion.

BM

Gustav Eberlein (1847–1926)

Boy Removing a Thorn, 1879–86
Marble, 61 1/2 x 22 1/2 x 30 3/4 in.
Acquired 1887

Although clearly harking back to its precursor in antiquity, a whole variety of features ensure that this figure by Eberlein transcends the level of a traditional genre piece and rises to that of a bacchic symbol. The youth is seated on an amphora with a relief depicting the ecstatic procession of the Bacchantes to the feast of Dionysus, and there are further motifs from the world of the god of wine: the goatskin, the wreath of grapes and wine leaves in the youth's hair, as well as the festoons and bukranias on the wooden plinth. This work unites late classical traditions, veristic detail, and technical perfection.

BM

Adolf von Hildebrand
(1847–1921)

Resting Shepherd Boy, 1871–73
Marble, 41¼ x 26¾ x 41¾ in.
Acquired 1903

A shepherd boy resting on a rock is
sleeping lightly. His limbs seem slack:
his left arm has sunk down, the right is
draped loosely around his crook, his
legs are set one in front of the other in
a relaxed manner, his head is resting for-

wards on his chest. This
interplay produces many
intriguingly different views,
and yet the expression of the
boy's dreamy isolation from
the out-side world is equally
strong from all angles.

When the figure was first
shown in 1873, it was a huge
success by virtue of its seemingly classical serenity, its
new-fashioned, generalizing
treatment of the human
form (without painstaking
naturalism), and its outstanding sculptural technique.
Conrad Fiedler, a friend of
Hildebrand's, wrote that the
latter's works expressed only
what was "purely and genu-
inely artistic, they are simply
true, unfalsified works of art,
and that is what separates them from all
the rest of contemporary, so-called
artistic activity."   BM

Adolf von Hildebrand
(1847–1921)

Dionysus, c. 1900
Marble, 57¼ x 57 x 6½ in.
Private loan

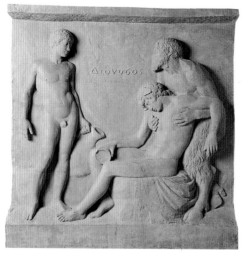

In its composition, this
work goes back to Greek
tomb reliefs, which show
the deceased
in a sitting position, often
in the company of relatives
bidding their last farewell:
thus Hildebrand's work
points towards death. On
the other hand, the subject
is Dionysus, the god of
exuberant festivals and of
the joys of life and wine.
The youth on the left may
be taken to be Ganymede,
while a goat-footed Silenus
approaches the intoxicated
bacchant from the right.
Thus the composition

links the joys of life with thoughts of death.

In this work, Hildebrand draws on an almost ascetically disciplined sculptural language, arranges his figures across the plane of the relief, builds up the composition with right angles, horizontals, and verticals, and conveys the underlying mood by gesture alone.

BM

Adolf von Hildebrand
(1847–1921)

Youthful Man, 1881–84
Marble, 72 x 26 ¹/₂ x 19 in.
Acquired 1885

Free from literary allusion, particular attributes, or genre-like gestures, a life-size young man stands in total harmony with himself, perfectly self-contained, outwardly unmoving and inwardly unmoved. In Hildebrand's own words, this person "wants nothing, does nothing and simply, I do believe, enjoys merely existing." The young man's spirit transcends the limitations of his solid, earthbound body; his sensibilities are not held back by materiality. Thus the figure portrays a well proportioned human body, but at the same time symbolizes far-reaching liberty and, by this, a kind of inner freedom that derives from the concord of body and spirit. In his inwardness — he is neither a concrete individual nor a particular type — he embodies the detached unworldliness of German idealism. The figure has its own philosophical rigor in that it clearly expresses Hildebrand's artistic striving for the ultimate formal purity of neoclassicism. It seems that the uniqueness of this figure must have impressed Reinhold Begas, the successful neo-Baroque sculptor who declared — against the resistance of many of his contemporaries — that the Nationalgalerie should purchase this work. The modernity of this work in the time it was created can only be fully appreciated when one considers how long neo-Baroque sentimentalism was to continue in sculpture and, for example, that

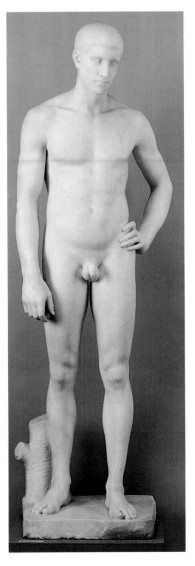

it was around 1900 when Begas created his monumental series of Hohenzollern statues for the Siegesallee in the Tiergarten in Berlin.

BM

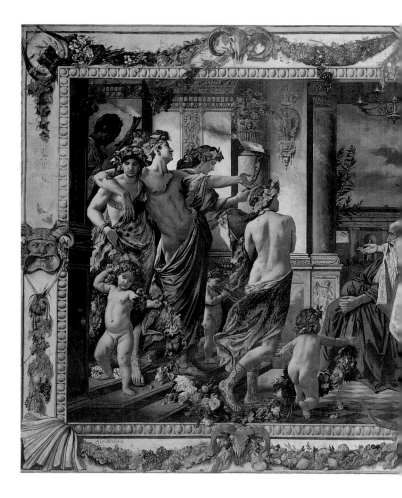

Anselm Feuerbach   (1829–1880)

The Symposium, Second Version,
1871–1873/4
Oil on canvas, 157 1/2 x 295 1/2 in.
Acquired 1878

"Agathon's friends have gathered in his
house in order to celebrate his winning
the prize as the best writer of tragedies...
While they indulge after the meal in
witty and high-spirited exchanges about
Eros, the mightiest and most splendid of
the gods, an intoxicated and euphoric
Alcibiades appears, returning with a
bacchic retinue from another feast. He
has come to crown the poet, who welcomes him as a friend." This was how
Henriette Feuerbach described the
work's theme which was taken from

Plato's philosophical dialogue, *The Symposium*. But the real focus of the composition is Socrates, as he quietly turns
away from the scene. The tension
between sensual pleasure and philosophical speculation is clearly demonstrated in the contrast between the two
halves of the picture. Crowned with a
laurel wreath, the host stands in the center, uncertainly linking the two.

A late manifesto of classical German
ideals of culture, a design for an epoch
— the apogee of Greek culture — and
a subjective confession, an example of
monumental art that can only find a
home in a museum: *The Symposium*
occupied Feuerbach for twenty years.
After his original idea from 1854, the
composition must have existed in broad

outline by 1860. Five years later, a large colour sketch was finished; the first large-scale version took from 1867 to 1869 (Karlsruhe, Staatliche Kunsthalle). Reactions were divided: people were put off by its cool colours as much as by the "ugly" realism of the figures.

The second version which Feuerbach then embarked on is much richer in its emphatically *Gründerzeit* (the decades after 1870) neo-Baroque architecture, decorative detail, and costume. The garland of flowers carried by the children is an addition and is echoed in the garlands of fruit on the painted frame which was also added at this stage.

However, the new motifs are not there simply to enrich the effect, for they are all symbolic of ancient tradi-

tions of making offerings, with specific reference to the cult of Dionysus, and underline the work's various allusions to the Dionysian. These are concentrated in the figure of Alcibiades, with whom Feuerbach himself identified. The contrast of Alcibiades' vitality and Agathon's formal, spiritual appearance portrays the inner conflict suffered by the artist, by art, and by civilization as a whole.   *CK*

up by having completed two major works, the second version of *The Symposium* and his second *Battle of the Amazons*.

His plain, collarless garment looks like a studio overall, and yet there is nothing bohemian about the appearance of this well-groomed, extremely self-aware, handsome man. Venetian portraits of the late Renaissance have clearly not only influenced the work's formal simplicity, whose very calm lends authority to the distinct movement of the head, and where the background is only interrupted by the edge of one wall: the fine grey coloration of the work also derives from Venetian precursors. *CK*

Anselm Feuerbach (1829–1880)

Self-Portrait, 1873
Oil on canvas, 24 ½ x 19 ¾ in.
Acquired 1899

Feuerbach's striking preference for self-portraits in a proudly distant pose — often with a cigarette — is not merely due to personal vanity: it also expresses the artist's claims to social acceptability on the grounds of the aristocracy of the intellect. Feuerbach painted this self-portrait at the age of forty-four, buoyed

Anselm Feuerbach (1829–1880)

Ricordo di Tivoli, 1866–67
Oil on canvas, 76 ½ x 51 ½ in.
Acquired 1902

"Inspired in its nonchalance and tenderness": the artist's own assessment of this painting even while he was still working on it. It is a lyrical work where there is a close relationship between the individual and the landscape, and where there is also a marked contrast between dreamy absorption and the contemplation of the outside world.

The singularity of this relationship becomes clear when one recalls, for example, Caspar David Friedrich's small figures which are turned away from the viewer as they gaze into the distance. Feuerbach's figures, on the other hand, occupying the picture plane like stage characters, achieve the same effect.

In Feuerbach's works children, naked like putti and heroic, or, as here, in countrified costumes — in any case always with beautiful, idealized southern looks — represent the purity of an existence close to nature. Soon after this, Feuerbach painted a second version of this composition for Count Schack in Munich, and several similar motifs are found elsewhere in his work. *CK*

Hans von Marées (1837–1887)

Self-Portrait with Yellow Hat,
1874
Oil on canvas, 38¼ x 31½ in.
Acquired 1935/2000

Facing the viewer with scarcely
disguised directness — like Dürer's
famous, Christ-like self-portrait in
Munich — with an expression of almost
foreboding seriousness, his stick across
his lap like a riding whip, lordly, unap-
proachable: the thirty-seven-year-old
presents himself more like a nobleman
or Grand Inquisitor than like an artist.
He wants to be perceived as the guar-
dian of a higher law corresponding to
the concept of art that he lived by,
which rises above the contingencies
of society and daily life. At the time,
Marées was living with his younger
friend, the sculptor Adolf Hildebrand,
in the former Monastery of San Frances-
co near Florence, which is alluded to in
the Tuscan landscape in the background.
The Naples fresco was just finished, and
the unapologetic assurance with which
it was created still sets the mood in the
Berlin portrait despite its dark, matt
coloration.   *CK*

Arnold Böcklin (1827–1901)

Self-Portrait with Death Playing the
Fiddle, 1872
Oil on canvas, 29½ x 24 in.
Acquired 1898

We will never know for certain whether
or not the personification of death was
an afterthought, as one account would
have it. Artists' self-portraits with a
memento mori have been known since
time immemorial. The inspiration for
this figure of Death playing the fiddle
probably came from the *Portrait of Sir
Bryan Tuke* in the Alte Pinakothek in
Munich, where Böcklin had lived since
1871. At the time it was wrongly attributed to Hans Holbein the Younger,
whose woodcuts of dances of death
with images of Death playing the fiddle
would also have been known to
Böcklin. In this self-portrait, Death is

playing on the lowest string, tuned to G,
which is here also the only string of the
fiddle. The painter, alert, has paused
in his work. According to the story,
Böcklin only painted in the figure of
Death in response to his friends' asking
what he seemed to be listening to. This
clearly relates to the search for the ultimate that characterizes this self-portrait,
and the inspiration the artist draws from
the constant proximity of death. The
impressive quality of this self-portrait
inspired other painters including Hans
Thoma and Lovis Corinth to paint similar portraits of themselves.   *AW*

Arnold Böcklin   (1827–1901)

The Isle of the Dead, 1883
Oil on wood, 31 1/2 x 59 in.
Acquired 1980

Arnold Böcklin spent the autumn of
1879 on Ischia. The Castello Alfonso,
on a small island nearby, deeply impressed him during his stay. When the
young, widowed Marie Berna visited
Böcklin's studio in Florence in 1880 and
asked for a "picture to dream by," the
memory of that landscape must have
merged with earlier memories of, for
example, the islands of the dead like San
Michele in Venice and Etruscan cliff-
necropolises. *The Isle of the Dead* became
one of Böcklin's most popular pictorial
works. He achieved this by combining a
limited number of ideas into an impressive atmospheric composition. The
motifs — island, water, and castle or villa by the sea — are already familiar from
many of his earlier works. However, in
this case they have been concentrated
into a statement of the artist's *Weltan-
schauung*. The location is sinister. The
viewer's gaze is led up the steps but can

penetrate no further into the darkness.
The island's strict symmetry, the calm
horizontals and verticals, the circular
island surrounded by high cliff walls,
and the magical lighting create an
atmosphere that is both solemn and sublime, evoking a sense of stillness and
other-worldliness. The ripple-less surface of the water and the boat bearing
the coffin with a figure shrouded in
white behind it add a melancholy tone
to the whole. The picture owned by the
Nationalgalerie is the third of five versions. It was commissioned in 1883 by
the art dealer Fritz Gurlitt. It was Gurlitt
who then gave the work its memorable
title and, with a keen eye for business,
asked Max Klinger to make an etching
of it. This was the version that established the extraordinary fame of the picture in the late nineteenth century. All-
pervasive in the form of photographs
and prints, the Isle of the Dead mirrored
the feeling of a whole epoch: people
identified with it and it became a favorite *fin de siècle* image.   *AW*

1801 but quickly became popular as the dangerous temptress on the rocks high above the Rhine. Romantic water spirits, nymphs, and mermaids populate nineteenth-century art and literature. Böcklin himself stated that in this work he wanted to translate the acoustic phenomenon of the breakers into painting. What may be sensed through the represented landscape is personified in the figure of the woman with the harp, which has strings that are not only very long and strong, but are all the same length — "For the sound of the breakers is always the same," as Böcklin explained to a friend in 1879 (Böcklin was presumably thinking of a so-called aeolian harp). A similar representation of the sounds of the sea is the subject of the picture *Triton, Blowing on a Shell* (1879–80). In its format and composition, and above all in the figure of the Triton, turning to the left, it could be a companion piece to *Ocean Breakers*.

AW

Arnold Böcklin
(1827–1901)

Ocean Breakers
(The Sound), 1879
Oil on wood,
47³/₄ x 32¹/₄ in.
Acquired 1897

The sea features as a motif in Böcklin's work after the 1870s. It is always inhabited by creatures from mythology — Naiads, Tritons, Nereids. He had already painted a work called *Ocean Breakers* in 1877 with a stylized, more schematic female figure (now in the Kunsthaus, Zurich) which bears a striking formal resemblance to one on an engraving by Salomon Gessner: *Melida, Yearning, with her Sheep on the Lonely Island*. Both works have clear echoes of the Lorelei of Clemens Brentano's novel *Godwi*, who only came into being in

Hans von Marées (1837–1887)

Saint George, 1880–82
Oil on wood, 71 x 41¼ in.
Acquired 1907, gift of Adolf von
Hildebrand

During the last years of his life, Marées
worked simultaneously on four monu-

mental three-part paintings. One of
these, formerly in the Nationalgalerie,
has been lost since 1945; the three
others are owned by the Neue Pinakothek in Munich. *The Three Riders* is the
only one of the four that recalls the
religious origins of the triptych, with its
depictions of St. Martin, St. Hubert,
and St. George, showing three forms of
virtue. The picture in the Nationalgalerie is the one remaining wing of a first
version of this work.

By slaying the dragon, the Roman
soldier, George, liberated a town whose
residents then had themselves baptized
to express their gratitude. Marées, who
had been trained in Berlin and Munich
as an equestrian and military artist, considered that the horse on the first version of the triptych was "rather like a
rocking horse" — perhaps referring to
the almost abstract play of the diagonal
lines, and the strict, relief-like plasticity
of the rider, who seems to glow against
the evening landscape with the intense
colours of a stained glass window. In a
smaller work in the Nationalgalerie,
Marées painted the dragon-slayer with
his own features.   CK

Hans von Marées (1837–1887)

Three Youths in an Orange Grove,
1878–83
Oil on wood, 39 x 25½ in.
Acquired 1919

Scenes and situations that could be
identified as historical events do not
form part of Marées mature output.
The configuration here of people in a
timeless landscape that relies for its
structure on the trunks of trees, is
expressing basic human situations: youth
and manhood, activity and contemplation. In this work, the estrangement of
humanity and nature seems to have been
resolved. Each position and movement
of the figures serves to integrate them
into a rationally ordered composition of
horizontals, verticals, and diagonals.
Nevertheless the atmosphere is lyrical,
conveyed by the evening twilight, in
which the colours — layer upon layer,

with the topmost layer applied fluidly and freely, as in a sketch — seem to glow with seemingly unfathomable depths. *CK*

Hans von Marées (1837–1887)

The Rowers, 1859
Oil on canvas, 65 $\frac{1}{2}$ x 53 $\frac{1}{2}$ in.
Acquired 1907

The start of Marées' mature period was marked by his one and only fresco cycle. At a center for marine zoology founded by the Darwinian Anton Dohrn not far from Naples, there was a room used during the day for study and in the evenings for social events. Together with the young sculptor Adolf Hildebrand, who made the frames, Marées created nine frescos to cover all four walls. Instead of the expected mythological and allegorical scenes, they were devoted to images of the landscape and day-to-day life of the surrounding area: fishermen setting out from the coast by Ischia, the circle of friends and artists around Dohrn in front of an *osteria*, people in an orange grove. Wide picture spaces, narrative abandoned in favor of timeless calm, seriousness and simplicity of concept and composition, the search for stature and relevance: this approach took subject matter that was normally only considered worthy of genre painting and raised it to the level of the ideal. The frescos were finished within the space of one summer. Preparations took the form, among other things, of large colored sketches that were drawn from life while the relevant section of the fresco was already being plastered; these then had to be painted with extreme rapidity while the skim was still wet. On the finished fresco, the group of rowers ended up in the corner of a section intended for a portrayal of the sky but where the rowers, however, dominate by virtue of the dynamic of their parallel diagonals. Marées left the thirteen large oil sketches behind in Naples as being of no further interest; it was only after his death that Hildebrand saw to their safekeeping, giving five to the Nationalgalerie. *CK*

wards, feeling their way to the figure — the compositional simplicity and rigor of the solid frontal view takes on an aspect of contained vitality that does not define at first, but which comes to life as the picture is viewed. Not understood by Leibl's contemporaries and caught in critical cross-fire because of its orientation towards French painting at the time of the Franco-Prussian War, Leibl's early work only received recognition in the early twentieth century when it was seen, in the context of Impressionism, as the guiding light for a new epoch.

AB

Wilhelm Leibl (1844–1900)

Portrait of Mayor Klein,
c. 1871
Oil on canvas, 34 1/4 x 26 1/2 in.
Acquired 1906

Leibl, a pupil of Piloty's, painted this early portrait of his brother's father-in-law shortly after his return from Paris. In its rejection of idealism and with its free brushstrokes, it is clearly a reaction to the work of Courbet. As the viewer becomes aware of the apparent fragmentation of the background through short, thick, slightly uneven brushstrokes — mostly calm diagonals leading down-

Wilhelm Leibl (1844–1900)

Two Heads (The Poachers), Fragment,
c. 1882–86
Oil on canvas on wood, 21 3/4 x 16 1/2 in.
Acquired 1899

The drama of this work's creation may be guessed at from the fact that it is the result of a larger work being cut up. This had been Leibl's largest and most dramatic work. Intending to escape from "the Holbein manner," Leibl planned a work that would allow him to depict movement, passion, and excitement. The work's program led by way of numerous preparatory studies to a radical change in style: smoothly applied paint is replaced by broad, energetic brushstrokes which show the angularity of the young man's features to be an expression of anger. Avoiding any binding details that might indicate a sense of time, Leibl simplified the image, heightening its power by the use of stark contrasts of light and dark and through the seeming infinitude of the two mens' gaze. Corinth, who viewed the picture in Paris just after its completion, and as yet uncut, saw in it what he called a "*furor teutonicus.*" Nevertheless, for Leibl himself, the work's unsuccessful spatial structure merely demonstrated the discrepancy between his aims and his abilities.

AB

Wilhelm Leibl   (1844–1900)

Dachau Woman and Child, 1873/74
Oil on panel, 33 ³/₄ x 26 ³/₄ in.
Acquired 1904

When Leibl painted the miller's wife of Plon during his stay in Grasslfing near Dachau in 1873/74, his copy of a painting in the Alte Pinakothek in Munich, *Charlotte Butkens and her Son* by Cornelis de Vos must have been in the forefront of his mind. While the woman from the Dachau countryside is less splendidly dressed, her dark costume provided an opportunity to depict a wide variety of textures and colour nuances. The plainer model actually suited Leibl's concept of 'honesty' better, and her monochrome dress allowed him to emphasise the intrinsic value of the painted picture plane. In both cases the mother is rather reserved while the child is more open about confronting the viewer. "The composition of the heads and the hands is very beautiful; it gives the picture an architectural strength. Some viewers might like to ask: 'Where is the spiritual element in this kind of painting?' The answer should be: 'It is in the still-life-like condition of the figures depicted, or if you prefer: in the cosmic still-life-like element of any image.'" (Karl Scheffler)

AW

Carl Schuch (1846–1903)

Still Life with Partridges and Cheese,
c. 1885
Oil on canvas, 30 x 24³/₄ in.
Acquired 1907

With complete disregard for public success and the art market, the Viennese painter Carl Schuch, who joined the circle around Leibl in 1870, produced a series of still lifes in which he pursued his investigation of artistic means. He translated visual perception into a system of tonal values and applied this to the picture as a whole. Thus the medium of painting — the colour material, the *alla prima* method, the structural nature of the brushstrokes, and the tectonics of the colour fields — all come to dominate so that objects lose their materiality. The sheer colour which glows from within disperses form and space alike. Painting as a generative process: after Schuch's death this concept of the visual led to his recognition in the Centenary Exhibition of 1906 as the modernist that he was.   *AB*

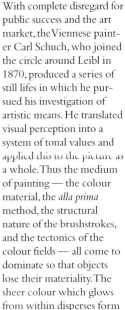

Louis Eysen
(1843–1899)

The Mother
of the Artist, c. 1877
Oil on canvas,
21¹/₄ x 16¹/₂ in.
Acquired 1901, gift from
M. Levy, Berlin

The Frankfurt landscape artist Louis Eysen also left some portraits. He was a member of the circle that gathered around Wilhelm Leibl; in 1869–70 he was in Paris with Leibl. For Eysen, Courbet's landscape painting was a revelation, but as a portraitist it would seem that Degas was his main inspiration. In Edgar Degas' portraits, sitters are also seen at extremely close quarters from a slightly raised view-

point, and his portraits would appear to have been similarly cropped, with the sitter off-center as though this were pure chance. Yet the figure is firmly secured in her setting by the linear structure of the composition. *AW*

Wilhelm Trübner (1851–1917)

On the Sofa, 1872
Oil on canvas, 20 1/2 x 17 3/4 in.
Acquired 1899 from the artist

Various influences combine to make a masterpiece of this inspired youthful work by the Munich artist Trübner. There are signs of the highly developed painterly techniques of the Leibl School and also of Dutch style. It seems likely that Danish Biedermeier also had a role to play in this. The truly modern aspect of this work is the emphasis on the picture planes. Thus the woman's dark dress spreads out like a dark stain with colours and objects grouped around it in decorative harmony. The sitter's expressionless face is visually no more important than her hands or the bread she is holding. Trübner was able to study this kind of close, frontal view and direct observation in Leibl's work (he had recently acquired a similar portrait from Leibl) and also in that of Courbet, who first exhibited in Munich in 1869 and who deeply impressed Leibl and his friends and colleagues. *AW*

Wilhelm Trübner   (1851–1917)

The Herreninsel Monastery at the
Chiemsee, 1874
Oil on canvas, 30 x 35 3/4 in.
Acquired 1897 from the artist

"In the summer Schuch was always
gripped by an irresistible longing for
landscape painting and so we decided to
make a tour of inspection of the island
of Rügen, travelling through the Harz
mountains and the Bavarian Forest and
finishing at the Herreninsel on the
Chiemsee." Trübner had become
friends with the painter Carl Schuch in
Munich in the winter of 1870–71. On
their summer trip in 1871 they hap-
pened to meet Wilhelm Leibl who
looked at their work and who soon
became an artistic role model for them.
Leibl gave Trübner sound advice, sug-
gesting he leave the academy and con-
centrate with other like-minded artists
on a detailed study of nature. Like
the other painters in the Leibl circle,
Trübner favored the *alla prima* method,
applying thick brushstrokes "wet on
wet" directly to the canvas, creating
works with a wide range of tonal values.

In the summer of 1874 at the Chiemsee,
Trübner, who had previously concentrated on figures and still lifes, now discovered for himself the artistic potential of the landscape. From this point
onwards, his preferred motifs were shady
groups of trees, the calm grounds of
country estates, and old, sprawling
buildings. His first attempts in this field
were emphatically coolly-factual, as
Lovis Corinth reported: "He spurned
everything that might please his public
or even his colleagues. While his paintings were outstanding for their tonal
beauty and purely painterly effect, there
were also so immensely serious that the
viewer was initially forced to reject
them." However, this does not apply to
*The Herreninsel Monastery on the Chiem-
see*. With the flat, muted green and
brown colour carpet of the sloping
meadow, the imposing building seen
from below, and the silvery sky up above
the high line of the horizon, this painting, along with the rest of the Herren-
chiemsee pictures of 1874, is one of the
best examples of this artist's somewhat
uneven output.   *AW*

Hans Thoma   (1839–1924)

Bouquet of Wild Flowers, 1872
Oil on canvas, 30 1/4 x 21 3/4 in.
Acquired 1916

A challenging motif in the form of a
multi-colored, mixed bunch of wild
flowers is represented here simply and
without sentimentality. In the spring
of 1868, the painters Scholderer and
Thoma had visited Courbet in Paris and
enthusiastically attended an exhibition
of his works. With Courbet's still lifes
fresh in his mind, on his return to
Munich Thoma painted a series of
flower pieces with free, fluid brushstrokes and dark backgrounds. On the
table there are usually additional items
— glasses, books, cups — which add an
element of narrative that distinguishes
Thoma's work from that of his role
model.   *AW*

Hans Thoma   (1839–1924)

Summer, 1872
Oil on canvas, 30 x 41 in.
Acquired 1926

The glowing deep blue sky lends the
painterly opulence of this hillside meadow and trees an air of unreality, and it is
only on closer observation that we see
that the couple with a lute in the grass
are wearing Renaissance clothing: thus
the painting is clearly more than a mere
portrayal of nature. The dancing cupids
in the sky, which may at first pass for
clouds, add to the dream-like quality of
the picture. Böcklin's influence is particularly evident here, although more
for his use of colour than for his mythological motifs.   *AW*

Karl Buchholz (1849–1889)

Spring in Ehringsdorf, c. 1872
Oil on canvas, 23³/₄ x 19¹/₄ in.
Acquired 1906

Karl Buchholz's landscapes are out-standing examples of the work by artists from the Weimar school of painting, which began to focus on this genre soon after its founding in 1860. Buchholz, who died young at age forty, is known above all for his poetic portrayals of typical Thuringia landscapes worked with a fine, soft brush. His main concern was not to reproduce large-scale, topographically exact views, nor was his interest in the heroic. Instead his aim was to depict the picturesque details of typical corners of the area. He observed atmospheric conditions and characteristic light effects with great sensitivity. His approach first comes properly into its

own in this picture of Oberweimar with its spring light and clear colours, combining the linearity of the branches with the painterly effect of the blossoms. In this, as well as in the unconventional angle of the view, Buchholz shows how close he was to the early plein-air painters. The intimacy of the small format matches the artist's choice of an unspectacular theme that, without historical allusions or props, is worthy of representation by virtue of its mood and light alone.

BM

Christian Rohlfs (1849–1918)

The Road to Gelmeroda, 1893
Oil on canvas, 21³/₄ x 24¹/₂ in.
Acquired 1934

Gelmeroda, a village near Weimar, has attracted painters since the nineteenth century, up to and including Lyonel Feininger. Rohlfs does not depict the village with its pointed spire, but shows instead the broad sweep of the road, flooded with wintry light as it snakes into the distance between meadows, gardens, and trees. The two incidental peasant figures seen from behind create a sense of depth that underlines the wide open spaces of the district. The paint is applied thickly in this work which is typical of Rohlfs' early manner. Later on his landscapes became much more Impressionist, and after experiments with abstraction he became one of the most important individualists among the Expressionists. In the end his work was classed as "degenerate" — a turn of events that is scarcely believable in the light of his work before 1900.

BM

Fritz von Uhde (1848–1911)

Grace before the Meal, 1885
Oil on canvas, 51¹/₄ x 65 in.
Acquired 1886

When Uhde painted his large-scale religious works *(Let the Little Children come unto Me)* which were popular around 1900, they seemed to some,

including the emperor, to be revolutionary in their approach. Biblical events are depicted in a contemporary setting; Christ appears as an individual. The social milieu is faithfully reproduced using the latest naturalistic techniques. There is no need for theological interpretation. The weight of the subject matter, however, means that there is a tendency to overlook both the fine play of light and shade in Uhde's works and the rich tonal modulations of his highly sophisticated plein-air paintings. *AW*

Munkácsy's influence and turned to modern plein-air painting. As he worked from nature his colours became brighter and purer. Uhde also followed Liebermann's lead in terms of subject matter, although his works are more anecdotal, and at first they were also more successful. *AW*

Fritz von Uhde (1848–1911)

Organgrinder in Zandvoort, 1883
Oil on wood, 18 1/2 x 14 1/4 in.
On loan from the Federal Republic of Germany

Uhde, who worked in Munich painting fashionable Dutch costume dramas, was inspired by Max Liebermann to go to Holland to study the people and the landscape on the spot. In the summer of 1882, he travelled to Zandvoort where he made studies for both versions of his composition of an organgrinder with children gathered around him. In Holland Uhde, like Liebermann before him, now left his dark studio, shaking off

Max Liebermann (1847–1935)

Women Plucking Geese, 1872
Oil on canvas, 47 x 67 ¼ in.
Acquired 1894, bequest of the artist's father,
Louis Liebermann

While he was still a student in Weimar,
Liebermann produced this early masterpiece. Although still showing the influence of other artists, nevertheless it also
points towards the future. In 1871 Liebermann, along with Theodor Hagen,
had visited the fashionable painter
Mihaly Munkácsy in Düsseldorf. In his
studio they saw his almost finished *Flax
Pickers*, which made a lasting impression
on Liebermann. When a friend returned from a study tour with a drawing of
women plucking geese, Liebermann
had found his subject, combining the
composition of the drawing with
Munkácsy's style. He made detailed
studies for the work in Weimar, taking
his own drawing of Goethe's last coach-
man as his model for the male figure —
Liebermann's lodgings as a student in
Weimar were opposite Goethe's house.
Women Plucking Geese was the first work
that the 25-year-old Liebermann exhibited, and it was not received well, being
mocked for its "poor" subject matter
and dark coloration. However, it did find
a buyer in the railway millionaire

Bethel Strousberg, and with the money
it earned him Liebermann travelled to
Paris where he had his first sight of
paintings by Millet and Courbet.   *AW*

Max Liebermann (1847–1935)

The Flax Barn at Laren, 1887
Oil on canvas, 52³/₄ x 91 in.
Acquired 1889

The Flax Barn at Laren is one of Liebermann's main works among his large-
scale paintings of groups of people and
workers from the 1880s. At the time,
Holland was an important destination
for Liebermann and his contemporaries.
They saw Rembrandt and Frans Hals as
their artistic role models, and by working directly from observation of their
subjects, they learned to leave their dark
studios and to shake off the fetters of
Munkácsy's working methods. In addition, in Holland they found the ideal of
a bourgeois society and a solid social
structure put into practice. At the time,
plein-air painting was still confusingly
modern, but *The Flax Barn at Laren* was
all the more offensive for the scale of
development of its subject matter. In a
bright, low, yet extensive shed, all the
figures are performing the same task,
spinning flax. By the wall under the
windows, there are children using fly-
wheels to wind the flax onto spindles.
Women and girls stand spaced throughout the room, each with a bundle of flax
under her arm, spinning the thread with
her hands. The scene is marked by its
strong, even rhythm; in their structure
the parallels of the floorboards and the
beams strengthen the harmony of the
work. The women stand in the space like
"pillars." The work depicts the calm of
everyday life — and a sense
of permanence in the monotony of
constantly repeated movements. The
colours are also without dramatic contrasts, reserved and cool. That peculiarly
Dutch, pale, silvery-grey light, which
Liebermann loved so much, permeates
the scene. Above all it is the light here, in
all its various reflections, that underlines
the life and beauty of the scene — an
everyday poem, calm and composed.

AW

Max Liebermann (1847–1935)

Cobbler's Workshop, 1881
Oil on wood, 25 ¼ x 31 ½ in.
Acquired 1899

In Dongen in the summer of 1881, Liebermann painted his *Cobbler's Workshop*,

completing it in two weeks. He had
already seen the workshop and had
decided to paint it a year before. During
the winter he had made an oil study,
followed by studies of models . Now he
returned well prepared, with a suitable
wood panel, to revive his first, fresh

impressions. In 1882 he sent the painting to the Paris Exhibition. There it was bought by the singer and collector Jean-Baptiste Faure, from whom it was later acquired by the Nationalgalerie. Faure was an early promoter of French Impressionism. While Liebermann was not typical of the artists in his collection, the presence of this painting shows that, in this image of work drenched in light, Faure, the connoisseur, recognized Liebermann's incipient move towards the principles of Impressionism. There are no echoes here of the somewhat oppressive half-light of *Women Plucking Geese*. Light pours in through the window and visibly flows round figures and objects alike. *AW*

Max Liebermann (1847–1935)

Orphan Girls in Amsterdam
(Study), 1876
Oil on canvas, 26 ½ x 31 ½ in.
Acquired 1923

Liebermann spent the summer of 1876 in Holland. In Haarlem he copied paintings and details from paintings by Frans Hals, mainly his late works such as the *Women Regents of the Old Men's Alms House in Haarlem*. On his way home to Amsterdam one day he managed to glimpse the courtyard of the city's orphanage. He was fascinated by the lighting conditions and the colours: the dresses of the girls in the municipal colours of red and black harmonising with brick red and green, the play of light and the easy movements of the children in their enclosed sphere of activity. The similarity between their social situation and that in the 17th-century pictures he had just studied would also have struck him — his first drawing of the courtyard is on the back of one of his copies after Frans Hals. Liebermann produced an actual painting of the orphan girls later in his studio. Our oil sketch conveys the artist's first fresh impression very accurately. It was purchased by Wilhelm Bode, the future general manager of the Berlin museums, for his private collection. *AW*

Lesser Ury (1861–1931)

Estaminet — Flemish Tavern,
1884
Oil on canvas, 39 ½ x 20 ½ in.
Acquired 1923

Ury, an individualist among artists, painted this interior in Belgium after a long period in Paris — three years before moving to Berlin where he established himself as a painter of cityscapes. "Skilled in the use of his palette, yet with little creative power:" this assessment by his contemporaries points towards the independence with which Ury reacted to contemporary art. The duality of this work was a particular source of irritation, for it combined Impressionistic sensitivity to the phenomena of light and shade with geometric space and stereometric figures, which gave the subject matter a metaphysical quality that transcended the ordinary and everyday. *AB*

Camille Corot (1796–1875)

Seine Landscape near Chatou,
c. 1885
Oil on canvas, 14 1/2 x 25 1/4 in.
Acquired 1941

In contrast to the powerful realism of
light that characterized the first half of
his oeuvre, after 1850 much of Corot's
work was devoted to dream-like depictions of atmospheric evenings with
water reflecting mild light and subtle
transitions from silver-grey to green.
Even when particular places are portrayed — Chatou is not far from the
painter's parental home in Ville-d'Avray
— Corot still interpreted these, as he
himself said, "as much with my heart as
with my eyes." *CK*

Charles-François Daubigny
(1817–1878)

Spring Landscape, 1862
Oil on canvas, 52 1/2 x 94 1/2 in.
Acquired 1906

As did Monet a few years later, Daubigny
owned a small studio boat in which he
travelled along the Oise and the Seine
on the lookout for motifs. The pictures
painted from the river often have a
panoramic element. Daubigny liked to
complete even large paintings out of
doors; they thus make a more live impression than most of the works by the
Barbizon painters. The Impressionists
held him in high esteem as their precursor. He, in turn, as a member of the jury
in the Salon, defended their works. *AW*

Honoré Daumier (1808–1879)

Don Quixote and Sancho Panza,
c. 1866
Oil on canvas, 30$^3/_4$ x 47$^1/_4$ in.
Acquired 1906

After 1850, the caricaturist Daumier,
virtually unknown as a painter, repeat-
edly produced scenes from the parodic
courtly romance of Don Quixote and
his servant Sancho Panza. This mighty
work by the Spaniard Cervantes (1547–
1616) describes a series of timeless disas-
ters. The emaciated itinerant knight
Don Quixote, who seeks out noble
deeds but only succeeds in fighting
against windmills, is grotesquely heroic.
Since he takes his dream world for reality, the real world seems to him to have
been bewitched; he is unable to unite
the ideal and the real. Sancho Panza, on
the other hand, embodies prosaic reality.
The telling power of Daumier's paintings derives from his relaxed, expressive
style of painting. Daumier has no time
for the minutiae of narrative. In his
hands, Cervantes' characters are con-
densed and stylized by means of powerful gesture into "types" characterized
with penetrating accuracy.   *AW*

Constant Troyon (1810–1865)

Woodcutters, c. 1855
Oil on canvas, 16$^3/_4$ x 21$^3/_4$ in.
Acquired 1916

Troyon, Rousseau, Dupré, and others
painted in the woods around the village
Barbizon near Paris. In the center of this
picture, woodcutters are at work. The
colours of their clothing, a touch of red,
some blue, and a certain amount of
gleaming white, provide the necessary
colour accents to set off the nuances of
green and brown. This method occurs
frequently in the works by painters from
the Barbizon school. It is a typical scene
at the edge of a wood, neither sublime
nor mysterious, instead intimate and
remarkable in its coloration.   *AW*

Gustave Courbet (1819–1877)

The Weir at the Mill, 1866
Oil on canvas, 21 1/4 x 25 1/2 in.
Acquired 1896, gift of James Simon

Courbet, who had put on his own exhibition in Paris in 1855 with the title "Le réalisme" out of protest at the rejection of his works, is the link between the Barbizon school and French modernism. His modernity was not in his subject matter but rather in his innovative use of paint and colour. He was the first to be accused of "dirty painting," an accusation that was later to be levelled at his successors like Max Liebermann.

Courbet painted numerous landscapes, most frequently depicting the chalk cliffs of the Jura mountains and the river valley of the Loue near where he was born in Ornans. This sombre view of a weir was painted on a black ground in the new spatula technique developed around 1865, not with the glowing patches of colour of other works of the time, but with consistently subdued tones of green, blue, and brown. In 1864 Courbet spoke about this way of building up a picture out of darkness: "You are puzzled that my canvas is black. But nature without the sun is dark and black; I am doing what light does, all I do is lighten everything that stands out and the picture is finished." One of the main themes in Courbet's work is water with all its interpretative potential: moving or still, bubbling up as a spring, standing in a grotto, flowing

freely or breaking over itself as a wave. In his famous studio picture from 1855, Courbet portrayed himself working on a landscape. There again it is a region from the French Jura, with a cliff, water, and a mill.

AW

Gustave Courbet (1819–1877)

The Wave, 1870
Oil on canvas, 44 x 56 3/4 in.
Acquired 1906, gift of
Guido Henckel von Donnersmarck

Just as Kleist once described the *Monk by the Sea*, so too Cézanne described Courbet's *Wave* with an equal degree of understanding: "... the one in Berlin is wonderful, one of the wonders of this century, with much greater movement, much more tension, a more poisonous green and a dirtier orange than the one here [Musée du Louvre, Paris], with the foamy surf of the tide, which comes up from out of the depths of eternity, its ragged sky and its pallid precision. It is as though it were coming right at one, it makes one jump back in shock. The whole room is filled with the smell of the foam." In 1869 in Etretat, in a studio right by the sea, Courbet had studied breakers. He attempted to recapture their violence and monstrous power by means of radical pictorial methods. Contemporary critics also read a political message into his wave paintings of 1869–70, seeing them as republican agitation and as illustrations of the power of the people.

Romanticism had already taught viewers to understand simple portrayals of nature on a symbolic level. Here the single wave is like a small section of eternity, with the plunging water as a transient moment of permanence. The layered paint, applied with a spatula and smoothed out with a palette knife, gives the portrayal of the moving mass a kind of wall-like strength, and it was this same combination of transience and

permanence that the poet Baudelaire had already identified in Courbet's earlier work. *AW*

Constantin Meunier (1831–1905)

Miners Returning Home, c. 1897
Bronze in a Wooden Frame
Overall dimensions 26 1/2 x 36 1/4 x 2 1/4 in.
Acquired 1898

For a long time, Meunier planned a memorial dedicated to "Work" and showing large numbers of workers, but it was not to be realized during his lifetime. He constantly worked on figures of miners, dockers, and rural laborers, portraying their world in reliefs, statues, busts, and paintings, thus helping to establish the life of the proletariat as a subject fit for sculpture. His plans for a memorial led to this relief, which shows a group of miners returning from the pit carrying their tools and wearing their typical leather miners' hats. Although inherently athletic, here they

are blinded by their sudden return to daylight and have been reduced by the demands of intense physical labor to a kind of animal-like dullness. The pit workers are dramatically grouped close together at the front edge of the relief; far away in the background is the winding gear and a chimney belching smoke. Meunier's view of the workers speaks of his own respectfully appreciative empathy. Yet the social criticism implicit in this sentiment clearly questions rather than blames. *BM*

Claude Monet (1840–1926)

View of Vétheuil, 1880
Oil on canvas, 23 1/2 x 39 1/2 in.
Purchased 1896 with funds from a donation
by Karl von der Heydt

The *View of Vétheuil* is one of the first
acquisitions of modern painting made
by the new director Hugo von Tschudi
in Paris. Julius Meier-Graefe saw the
picture in March 1898 in the newly arranged halls of the Nationalgalerie and
noted: "This Monet seems to me the
most valuable of the French paintings.
It is a very rare picture; ... it is a delicate
Monet, but in its almost Rococo-like
delicateness of line and colour it has all
the irresistible infallibility of all the paintings by this master." By describing it in
unusual terms as "Rococo-like" Meier-
Graefe grasped a characteristic feature of
Monet's art around 1880. Both summer
and winter views of Vétheuil are distinguished by a new pastel-like colour-
fulness. The technique is livelier than in
the 1870s; decisive little coloured dashes
are evidence of the painter's firm sure
brushstroke. This gives some works an
almost decorative touch and makes
them seem oddly cheerful.   *AW*

Claude Monet (1840–1926)

St. Germain l'Auxerrois, 1867
Oil on canvas, 31 x 38½ in.
Acquired 1906, gift of Karl Hagen

In 1865 the young Monet had his first
works accepted by the "Salon des Beaux
Arts," the official show of art in Paris.
In 1867 his works were already being
refused. This was the time when Monet
and his friends were developing the
principles of Impressionism, a form of
painting that seeks to capture the first
"impression" of what the eye sees, and
which disappointed the public's precon-
ceived notions of how things actually
looked.

In April 1867, Monet and Renoir
had asked the board of the Louvre for
permission to put up their easels in the
columned passage of the Perrault Wing.
Looking out from this elevated position,
Monet painted three views of the city.
The view towards the Gothic Church
of St. Germain l'Auxerrois and the
surrounding residential area depicts
the solidity of the architecture, with
Monet handling its intricate bulk with
skill and artistry. At the same time, however, the blossoming chestnut trees and
the colored daubs representing people
walking about already point towards
Impressionism in its maturity.   *AW*

Claude Monet (1840–1926)

Summer, 1874
Oil on canvas, 22 ½ x 31 ½ in.
Acquired 1907, gift of Karl Hagen and
Karl Steinbart

In April and May of 1874, for the first time Monet and his artist friends exhibited their own works rejected by the official "Salon" in rooms belonging to the photographer Nadar on the boulevard des Capucines. A newspaper critic, referring to Monet's *Impression — Sunrise* of 1872 mockingly coined the term "Impressionists." Since these artists were, however, above all concerned to capture the visual appearance of reality, they themselves took this name on. The painters Renoir, Manet, and Monet spent their summers together in Argenteuil on the Seine and worked on perfecting their particular artistic style. Among the works that Monet produced in Argenteuil is this sun-drenched meadow with hazy mountains in the distance; a picture in which his wife Camille and his son Jean have no more visual presence than the wind-blown trees or the colored shadows on the grass. As the critic had correctly real-ized, Monet's interest was solely in conveying an impression. Later on, Paul Cézanne was to say to Ambroise Vollard that "Monet is simply an eye, but — by God — what an eye." The painting *Summer* was shown at the second exhibition at Nadar's in 1876. In his review of the exhibition, the writer Emile Zola singled out this work by Monet for particular praise. *AW*

Edouard Manet   (1832–1883)

The House at Rueil, 1882
Oil on canvas, 28 1/4 x 36 1/4 in.
Acquired 1906, gift of Karl Hagen

Edouard Manet's fascination with the effects of light and colour was constantly renewed as he took in the myriad impressions of the infinitely varied world around him. His portrayal of the house just outside Paris belonging to his host, the poet Eugène Labiche, was in no way intended as a faithful view. Instead he restricted himself to a section of the facade, like a detail, much in the style of Japanese woodcuts. It is not possible to take in the house as a whole, both because of the limited view and because of the tree trunk that calculatedly cuts through the aedicule and thus through the functional and aesthetic center of the house, heightening the viewer's attention and fascination. While the facade is bathed in blazing sunlight, one can nevertheless sense the cooling shade cast by the crown of the tree up above the top edge of the picture. One also senses that there is a slight breeze causing the patches of light to gently shift their position. "A blithe spirit has created this picture with consummate skill" (Hugo von Tschudi) — skill that is evident in the finely balanced play of colours, the powerful contrasts of red and green, and the restrained resonance of tones of yellow and blue.   *BM*

Edouard Manet
(1832–1883)

White Lilac, c. 1882
Oil on canvas,
21 1/4 x 16 1/2 in.
Acquired 1909, bequest of
Felicie Bernstein

This spray of lilac — as laconic as it is tonally fascinating — is one of a group of still lifes that Manet painted in the last years of his life as he was becoming increasingly ill. Manet's brush records with simplicity and sensitivity the transient effects of light on the tender pastel colours of the lilac, on the restless texture of the blossoms, and in the independent restlessness of the light refractions in the water. Decades before, he had devoted considerable painterly finesse to simple still lifes. But late works like this one, with its concentration on finely gradated colour combinations — blue, green, and brown — and on the meticulously observed materiality of the heavy flower heads, is pure painting, practised for its own sake and, in its concentration, bearing witness to the wise self-limitation of the mature, older artist.   *BM*

Edouard Manet (1832–1883)

In the Conservatory, 1879
Oil on canvas, 45 ¼ x 59 in.
Acquired 1896, gift of Eduard Arnhold,
Ernst and Robert von Mendelssohn, and
Hugo Oppenheim

Manet preferred compositions with two figures as opposed to the straightforward portrait form because it opened up the possibility of interesting dialogue situations. The double portrait of Jules Guillemet and his wife, painted in the conservatory of the painter Johann Georges Otto Rosen, is one of the most important of these works because of the sensitivity with which it uses the most delicate nuances of colours and contrasts to describe and re-connect the psychologically tense, only outwardly detached, relationship of the two figures. The theme of the picture is the interplay between the elegant lady — the owner of a fashion shop in Paris — and the gentlemen turned in her direction. He seems rather small due to the way he is bending over and brushes against the upper edge of the picture, while the feminine beauty with the effortless noblesse of her extended posture occu-

pies a large part of the picture space. Despite their being separated by the back of the seat — with its own graphic appeal by virtue of its transparency — the understated focal point of this rich conservatory scene with all its plant forms and subtle colours is the hands approaching each other.

Manet's paintings are fascinating for a variety of reasons: a palette of colours that is subtle yet not without the tension of contrast, plus subject matter that is free from literary or symbolic content. This is painting at its highest level, drawing on an uncommonly fertile imagination, on the constant awareness of visual phenomena, and on a gift for laconic observation that translates every sight into a subtly mediated experience for the eyes. Particularly in the compositions with two or more figures, there are also extremely skilfully dramatized scenes with psychologically intriguing configurations of actors or often of silent players, wordless and motionless like the different elements in a still life.

BM

Auguste Renoir (1841–1919)

Summer, 1868
Oil on canvas, 33 ½ x 23 ¼ in.
Acquired 1907, donation from Mathilde
Kappel, Berlin

Lise Tréhot, Renoir's mistress for several years, sat for him in various roles. On the one hand this portrait follows in the traditions of Romanticism with the sitter's blouse slipping from her shoulder — although without erotic coquettishness — with her dark, tangled hair and the open, frontal pose which still avoids eye contact with the viewer. On the other hand the powerful plasticity of the form shows the influence of Courbet. The sunlight flickering through the background foliage, rendered with its broad brushstrokes, does not reach the sitter, who is lit only by the light in the studio.   CK

Auguste Renoir (1841–1919)

Children's Afternoon at Wargemont, 1884
Oil on canvas, 50 x 68¼ in.
Acquired 1906, donation from the banker Karl Hagen, Berlin

In 1879 Renoir became a friend of the banker and diplomat Paul Bérard and his wife Marguerite. He painted portraits, still lifes and landscapes for them, and visited them both in Paris and in their chateau in Wargemont, where he painted the large picture of their daughters Marguerite, Lucie, and Marthe. Over a period of years he also painted them individually; but here the subjects are distanced from the viewer by being "arranged" as a genre piece — in the spirit of a convention going back over the centuries. The girls' faces are consciously juxtaposed as profile, three-quarter view, and front view. The work's precise linearity perfectly reflects the artist's "classicizing" phase, as does the shadowless intermingling of transparent tones, cool on the left and colorful on the right. The many different patterns, as on a Japanese woodcut, underline the unity of the picture surface. *CK*

Camille Pissarro (1830–1903)

Louveciennes with Mont Valérien in the Background, 1870
Oil on canvas, 17¾ x 21 in.
Acquired 1961 with funds from the German Lottery Foundation, Berlin

From 1869 until 1872 Pissarro lived in Louveciennes, a village to the west of Paris above the Seine. His friends Monet, Sisley, and Renoir came to visit him here. In this work, Pissarro has portrayed one of his everyday motifs — a scene near where he lived, applying the paint thickly and roughly, and demonstrating an honesty towards nature for which his colleagues respected and admired him. As many as thirty-four of these works date from 1870 alone. *CK*

Paul Cézanne (1839–1906)

Mill on the Couleuvre at Pontoise,
1881
Oil on canvas, 28 ½ x 35 ½ in.
Acquired 1897, gift of Wilhelm Staudt,
Berlin

Cézanne's art was still highly controver-
sial when the Nationalgalerie purchased
this painting: it was only two years previously that the French government had
accepted two of his works as part of the
Caillebotte donation, but had rejected
another three. For a long time, Cézanne
commuted between his place of birth,
Aix-en-Provence, and Paris, although
he also stayed in various towns of the
Ile-de-France. Camille Pissarro lived in
Pontoise northwest of Paris. Cézanne
paid him several visits there (the first in
1872, the last from May to October of
1881), and their work together encour-
aged him in the direction of light,
impressionistic colours: "We perhaps all
go back to Pissarro," he later said. The
older painter also led him to that clarity
and calm that pervade the painting of
the mill, and which are achieved despite
extraordinary accuracy in his portrayal
of the motif; this is clear from old pictures showing the Moulin des Etannets
on the rue des Deux Ponts, one of many
mills in that area that depended on the
corn trade for its existence.

The flat white houses in the background create a sober effect. At the same
time, there is a geometric order that
takes in the whole picture plane. The
composition is governed by strict horizontals and verticals cutting across each
other. Despite interruptions, these
apparently run as parallels throughout
the whole picture; closer examination,
however, shows that in the lower half
of the picture, that is to say in the foreground, they slope away increasingly into diagonals. The colours range through
shades of green to airy blue and ocher.
Since each brushstroke is independent
— whether short and straight or curved
or even curled — the paint does not
entirely cover the painting's ground,
thus incorporating its pale, immaterial
quality.   *CK*

Paul Cézanne (1839–1906)

Still Life with Flowers and Fruit,
c. 1888–90
Oil on canvas, 25 3/4 x 32 1/4 in.
Acquired 1906, gift of Robert
Mendelssohn

In the 1880s, Cézanne's work centered around still lifes. He produced over 170 paintings in this genre, with the same elements but rearranging them in order to arrive at new formal and painterly answers. A wooden table, a tablecloth, fruits, and a ginger jar were all items in his standard repertoire, with the addition here for the first time of a generous bunch of wildflowers — daisies, carnations, and poppies. None of Cézanne's other still lifes are so rich in decorative detail, yet the space retains its simplicity of character, and the work retains its formal rigor. The opulence of the right-hand side of the image is balanced by the dark background and the cool, white tablecloth. The individual objects are sensually portrayed and relate in a somewhat monolithic manner to each other and to the picture space. They are an expression of Cézanne's search for the being of things, which in itself comes through particularly in his style of painting. The surrounding space is divided into planes, but each is alive in every detail — permeated, dissolved, and reconstituted. The colours are of an infinite richness and vibrate in the juxtaposition of finely gradated light values and tones. The picture is notable for its cool, harmonious colour chords — green, yellow, and violet or red, white, and blue. Cézanne's constant rearrangements were made in an attempt to grasp and understand the objects. He consciously chose the diffuse light of the studio in preference to bright daylight in order to emphasize the sheer physicality of the objects. The objects in Cézanne's still lifes, whether for daily use, artificial, or natural, are detached from their normal function. Cézanne's still lifes reflect his recognition that there are laws governing the world and the portrayal of its complexity. *KS*

Edgar Degas   (1834–1917)

Dancer, Looking at the Sole of her
Right Foot, c. 1910
Bronze casting c. 1919–25
Bronze, black patina, 18 1/2 x 9 1/2 x 7 3/4 in.
Acquired 1926

Degas, the chronicler of pulsating city
life, was as much at home at racecourses
and in bars as in the world of the stage.
His wax and plaster sculptural studies
only became known after his death,
when they were cast in bronze. Many
are of dancers, either dancing or captured during the interval. The dancer
holding still to look at the sole of her
foot might recall the figure from
antiquity removing a thorn and its
various successors, but in antiquity, as in
Neoclassicism, an unstable composition
of this sort would have been unthink-
able, with only one uncertain support
and with the limbs directing energy
both out into space and back again. It
is precisely this unconventional aspect
of the work along with the impressionistic treatment of the surface that lends
Degas' sculptures their particular attraction.   *BM*

Edgar Degas   (1834–1917)

Prancing Horse, c. 1890
Bronze casting after 1917
Bronze, 100 x 10 3/4 x 5 in.
Received 1952

Like many of the wax models in Degas'
estate, this figure of a horse was in poor
condition since the artist himself paid
little attention to these works which did
not find favor among the critics. In
addition, without a conventional training as a sculptor, he did not have the
technical expertise to construct figures
that would last, and saw no value in perfecting his technique as a craftsman.
Thus the bronze casting shows the wire
underframe that supported the now
partially lost wax of the original. The
contrast between the more fragile parts
and the horse's solid body gives the figure an air of extreme light-footedness.
The weightless, playful overall impression is underlined by the head held
high. Despite the sheer physicality of
the prancing horse, the restless play of
light on its finely modelled surface
makes the creature seem somehow
immaterial — very much in the spirit of
the Impressionists' interest in momen-
tary visual perception. Degas clearly at-
tached greater importance to spontaneous sensual perception than to a detailed
description of the inner structure and
anatomical particularities of a figure. *BM*

Edgar Degas   (1834–1917)

Conversation, c. 1883
Pastel on card, 25 ½ x 34 in.
Acquired 1896, gift of
Oskar Huldschinsky

Two women are caught leaning over a table set at an angle while a third woman turns away in the background. The title, *Conversation*, has confusingly little to do with the scene, for any conversation between the three has long since come to a halt. Degas, a master of the fleeting impression, here creates a well-constructed composition from his subject matter, which has about it all the arbitrariness of a reportage snapshot: figures which are cut into, set against each other, and thus isolated, heads turned significantly away and obscured faces — Degas precludes insight into the women's silence. They are not together out of mutual understanding; instead there is a sense of meaningless waiting, a brooding atmosphere not conducive to conversation. While most Impressionist paintings live by the light of their colours, here — as in other pastels and oil paintings by Degas — the colours are markedly dull, in keeping with the gloomy interior and underlining the somber mood. The ground colour of the ocher card used and the matt effect of the pastel chalks suit the muted colours. The work is defined by tones of grey-green, grey-blue, and the greyish brick-red of the women's clothes, and is held together by the shades of ocher in their gloves and in the background.

Many of Degas' numerous pastels are as large as oil paintings. Thus the artist declared his own personal allegiance to this form that was somewhere between drawing and painting, and which had been out of fashion since the Rococo and *Empfindsamkeit* (the age of sentimentality). The Paris art dealer Durand-Ruel bought this work in 1883; he, for one, was clearly convinced that this pastel was equal to any oil painting.

BM

The introspective heaviness of the pose clearly sets the mental creative process apart from carefree poetic dreaming. Here the very earthbound quality of the physical being corrects the idealizing notion — prevalent since the *Sturm und Drang* — of the free flights of fancy of the creative genius, replacing it with an attitude that sooner reflects the fateful heaviness of human life and suffering. Rodin's *Thinker* was created as part of a larger project, *The Gates of Hell*, which he was commissioned to make in 1880. This sculpture was to be positioned at the top-center of *The Gates of Hell*, which was not cast until after Rodin's death; thus it was designed to be viewed from below. *The Thinker* was seen as a modern image of artistic creativity and became one of Rodin's best-known plastic works. A larger version is to be seen at Rodin's grave, recalling the sculptor's creativity, his concept of life as an artist, and one of his greatest works.   *BM*

Auguste Rodin   (1840–1917)

The Thinker, c. 1881–83
Bronze, 28 x 15 1/4 x 22 1/4 in.
Acquired 1905, gift of
Oskar Huldschinsky

This seated figure, resting his head on his hand, clearly demonstrates intellectual exertion through gesture and mime.

Auguste Rodin   (1840–1917)

Bust of the Sculptor Jules Dalou,
1884–89
Bronze, 20 1/4 x 19 3/4 x 9 1/4 in.
Acquired 1896, gift of Max Liebermann

Among Rodin's portrait busts, this one of his teacher Jules Dalou, with its proud, noble air, stands out particularly, combining the inspired individualism of one of the most successful sculptors of his age with the self-confidence of the artists of that time.   *BM*

Auguste Rodin (1840–1917)

Man and his Thought,
1899–1900
Marble, 30¼ x 18 x 21¾ in.
Acquired 1901, bequest of Felix Koenig

A bearded artist kneels reverently in front of his own creation, a dreamy, young female being. Both figures only emerge partially from the rock; the act of creation is not yet finished. The artist is breathing a soul into his invention: shades of Pygmalion as cold stone is laboriously imbued with warm-blooded life. The fragmented form with its phil-osophical significance and implications of endless toil is a fitting expression for a metaphor of genesis which includes the transient condition of incompleteness. Similar two-figure pieces occur throughout Rodin's work, demonstrating the complex inter-relationships of antagonism and concurrence, male and female, artist and muse, reverence and devotion, action and contemplation.

BM

Aristide Maillol   (1861–1944)

Eve with an Apple, 1899
Bronze, 22³/₄ x 8³/₄ x 5 in.
Acquired 1978

A nude female figure turns her head over her shoulder but does not look at the apple in her hand. The image may well evoke thoughts of the Fall from Grace and the forbidden fruit. The woman's hand is turned away in a distancing gesture. However, Maillol does not draw here on Christian visual traditions alone; there are equally strong associations with the judgement of Paris: it is as though Eve were also Venus, tempted and specially chosen at one and the same time.   *BM*

Vincent van Gogh   (1853–1890)

Le Moulin de la Galette, 1886
Oil on canvas, 15 x 18¹/₄ in.
Acquired 1929

In the 1880s, Van Gogh was still only setting out on his life as an artist and, after his drawing studies, turned in 1884 to the problem of painting. He studied Delacroix's writings on colour, Charles Blanc's *Grammaire des Arts du Dessin*, and experimented with the latter's theory of complementary colours. However, since he consciously chose to always mix his colours with black, his works turned out dark, almost monochrome. It was only having studied the works of Frans Hals in Amsterdam and of Rubens in Antwerp that he decided to juxtapose pure colour values. His aim, however, remained unchanged: not to imitate nature but "to create something new on a parallel colour scale." Van Gogh's brother Theo also criticized him for "painting things black" and pointed him towards the Impressionists, with whom he was just starting to do business in Paris.

One of Van Gogh's first "clear

colour" works was that showing the mill on Montmartre, which he painted shortly after his return to Paris in 1886. It is still somewhat muted, yet now pure red stands against green and blue against orange. The two years that Van Gogh then spent in Paris, studying trends in contemporary art as well as old Japanese woodcuts, ultimately led him to his own highly expressive, glowing use of colour.   *AW*

Medardo Rosso
(1858–1928)

Sick Man in
Hospital, 1889
Wax over plaster,
9 x 8 1/2 x 8 3/4 in.
Acquired 1972

As an autodidact, free from
the classical traditions of
nineteenth-century sculp-
ture, Medardo Rosso developed a language which
came close to the
Impressionists' manner of
seeing things: objects seem
insubstantial, without sharp
contours, and it is as though
they were only modelled by the play of
light. Physicality is dissolved by indeter-
minacy. Rosso spurns anatomic accuracy, leaving questions unanswered as in a
sketch. The impression of "decomposi-
tion" is in keeping with the *fin de siècle*
interest in the morbid. But Rosso's own
chosen motifs were also largely elegiac.
Here an old man, wrapped in blankets
and bowed down under a high fur hat,
sunk into himself under the weight of
old age or of his individual fate, holds
an unidentifiable object in his hands, and
it is almost as though a curse has trans-
fixed him in his high-backed armchair.
It must be for the viewer to decide
whether this might be a rabbi, a scholar,
or even a wizard. *BM*

from which Eurydice is freed. However,
since Orpheus, despite having been forbidden to do so, turns around to look at
Eurydice as she flees from Hades, he will
lose her again. The gravity and sadness of
the legend are set in the peaceful daily
life of the Breton coast with its swim-
mers and sailors, and ancient times and
the present mingle in a startling manner.
The familiar landscape is altered and
takes on an air of timeless grandeur. To
emphasize the picture plane, Denis, a
founding member of the group of sym-
bolist painters known as "Les Nabis"
(The Prophets), counteracts the impression of depth and permeates the colours
with light. Fauvism is clearly not far
away. *CK*

Maurice Denis
(1870–1943)

Eurydice, 1903/04
Oil on canvas, 29 3/4 x 46 in.
On permanent loan from the
Ernst von Siemens-Stiftung

Groups of figures dispersed
throughout the landscape
hint at the Orpheus legend:
a figure wearing a wreath
supports Orpheus' dying
lover; on the left, the fateful
snake is being killed. The pit
in the middle-ground
stands for the underworld

Max Klinger   (1857–1920)

Walker, 1878
Oil on wood, 14 1/2 x 34 in.
Acquired 1933

Treading the fine line between fantasy and reality, Klinger produced his first series of etchings in Berlin while at the same time painting this snapshot of social decay in the growing city that can be sensed nearby. Behind the long brick wall there will be a building site or factory. In front of it, the landscape is already ruined: a bleak void with hard, geometric boundaries that are only softened by the curve of a fence. A young man out for a walk, seeing himself threatened by members of a gang, is trying to defend himself and has drawn his pistol. The rhythmically varied distances between the figures and their harsh shadows underline their isolation. The somewhat sensational portrayal of tension seems, if anything, ironic.   CK

Anton von Werner   (1843–1915)

In the Troops' Quarters outside Paris, (October 24, 1870),
1894
Oil on canvas, 47 1/4 x 62 1/4 in.
Acquired 1894

This work goes back to Werner's time with a support command in Versailles twenty-four years earlier during the Franco-Prussian War. Protected by the court and specially chosen as the iconographer of the birth of the German nation as a state, Werner, who had been the director of the Art Academy since 1875, had meanwhile become the "Art Pope" of Germany in the late 1890s and provoked bitter opposition both from founders of the Secession and from dealers in international art. The picture shows German soldiers making music in the salon of an elegant chateau that they have requisitioned in Brunoy. Werner, like the "Landeskunstkommission" (Regional Art Commission), which purchased this work the same year it was painted, was well aware of the popularity of war pictures. But what becomes clear with hindsight is that the painting provides more than emotional relief: unintentionally, the discrepancy between the fine Second Empire interior and the rough behavior of the officers, including their attempts to be cultivated, in fact relativizes the victors' pathos.

AB

Max Klinger (1857–1920)

Amphitrite, 1895–99
Marble, eyes inlaid with amber,
70 1/4 x 18 1/2 x 16 1/2 in.
Acquired 1901, donated by the heirs of the banker Felix Koenig

The desire to transcend the boundaries between different art forms had led Klinger to sculpture. He returned from a visit to the Greek island of Syros with an old marble step from which he planned to sculpt a half-length figure; it was only while he was working that he decided to add the draped legs. The idea of calling her after the Greek sea-goddess, "the one surrounded by sea," may have come from the provenance of the stone. Contemporaries explained that the arms were missing because of the original dimensions of the stone, however there are other examples of Klinger's interest in the problems of the

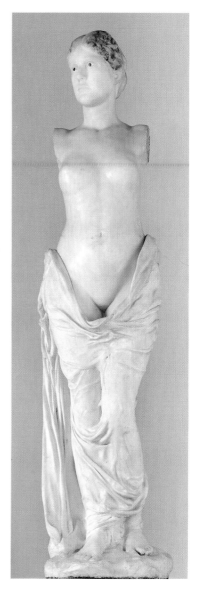

human torso, and in this he comes close to the pioneers of modernism. However, this emphasis on form and material runs contradictory to the lifelike, subtly naturalistic treatment of the flesh and the light, flowing draperies here — all the more so since Klinger replaces the physical ideals of classical sculpture with the features of a contemporary town-dweller.

CK

Ludwig von Hofmann
(1861–1945)

Dreaming, c. 1898
Oil on wood, 17³/₄ x 27³/₄ in.
Acquired 1972

Ludwig von Hofmann's idyllic, Arcadian landscapes reflect the Art Nouveau movement of around 1900. They are populated by walking, dancing, and dreaming figures. Decorative symbolism pervades these works, of the sort that Hoffmann had admired in the works of Puvis de Chavannes, Maurice Denis, and Albert Besnard in Paris.

The young woman in *Dreaming* is surrounded by the life element, water. The perfect profile of her head recalls portraits of women from the Florentine Renaissance. The overall impression of the picture is of something precious: it is painted with the finest modulations of colour on a wood panel that was cut to fit an old Italian frame. The young woman's features resemble those of "Flora" in Ludwig von Hofmann's engagement picture from the same year. The richly symbolic image seems also to be an illustration of a dream life. The bather's hair is decorated with a bluish poppy, an ancient symbol for sleep, but which here is also reminiscent of the blue flower of Romanticism. The cliff face by the sea contains a mysterious grotto, also a symbol of erotic fantasies since time immemorial. The picture space is enclosed by red tendrils, which could equally well be veins. This inclusion of the frame as part of the picture is typical of many Art Nouveau works.

AW

Franz von Stuck   (1863–1928)

Self-Portrait in the Studio, 1905
Oil on canvas, 28¹/₂ x 30 in.
On loan from the Federal Republic of Germany

In this work, Stuck declares himself to be an artist by including his palette, paintbrush, and the easel in the background. He has stopped painting for a moment to check what he has created, that is to say, not only the work in progress but also the interior of his Munich studio. He decorated his bourgeois artist's villa as a kind of all-embracing credo. Evidence of this can be seen below the Renaissance ceiling in the frieze of hunting centaurs (the centaur is a favorite motif in Stuck's paintings and sculptures because of its human-animal duality) and in the names of artists in whose footsteps Stuck felt he was following including Phidias, the most celebrated artist of antiquity, and Michelangelo. Thus

Stuck is measuring himself against one of the greatest geniuses of the Renaissance, and in fact — not without arrogance — also laid claims to the latter's universalism. As was often his custom, Stuck partly relied on photographs when he was working on this self-portrait, which he painted in the same year that he was elevated to the nobility. This self-portrait — imbued with pride and an element of pathos — is notable for the fact that the artist has emphatically portrayed himself from below, that is, raising himself up above the viewer. He is perfectly dressed and groomed: Stuck as the veritable "Prince of Painting" in Munich.

BM

Franz von Stuck   (1863–1928)

Sin, c. 1912
Oil on canvas, 34 ³/₄ x 20 ¹/₂ in.
On loan from the Federal Republic of
Germany (painting) and the
Villa Stuck Museum, Munich (frame)

The most notorious and, after the *Isle of the Dead* (p. 82), most popular work of art around 1900 was *Sin* by Franz Stuck. One of the first versions of it caused a great sensation at the Munich Secession exhibition in 1893. Stuck repeated the memorable picture with many variations up to 1912. Shining in the greenish darkness is the naked upper body of a woman, its brightness emphasized even more by her long dark hair, and twisting around her in a grand curve like a luxurious stole is a blue-patterned serpent. It stares at the viewer over the woman's shoulder in the same unfathomable way she does. On the subject of

this scintillating motif there exists a rather conventional note by Stuck on one of his drawings: "Sin / drawing you in with fiery eyes / lustfully flaunting white breasts / drawing you in with fiery eyes / the naked woman lures you to seduction, / but right next to her beside the alluring / face, the poisonous snake darts its tongue in and out." Stuck called a preparatory etching dating from 1891 *Sensuality*.

Several versions of *Sin* have a pseudo-antique gilt frame based on a design by Stuck featuring an aedicule with fluted pilasters to the right and left, and the large title incised clearly at the bottom. The frame underscores the laboured meaningfulness of the subject.   AW

Walter Leistikow   (1865–1908)

Lake Grunewald, 1895
Oil on canvas, 65 3/4 x 99 1/4 in.
Acquired 1898, donation of Richard Israel

"It is Leistikow's lasting achievement
— and will always remain so — that he
found a style that can express the melancholy charm of the surroundings of
Berlin. We see the Grunewald lakes and
those on the upper Spree through his
eyes; he has taught us to see their
beauty," said Max Liebermann in a
memorial speech honoring his friend.
For ten years they had led the Berlin
Secession together, which was founded
after *Lake Grunewald* had been rejected
by the "Great Berlin Art Exhibition" of
1898. This is the most successful of
many works with similar themes. Its
clear, expansive composition with the
dark, shadowy shape
of the woods against
the orange-yellow
of the evening sky,
repeated in the
water, lends this
work the stature of
a great landscape in
its own right. Its un-
usual angle and
expressive linearity
show the influence
of the Japanese
woodcuts Leistikow
had admired during
his stay in Paris in
1893. The clear con-
tours of the forms

and the stark con-
trasts are reminiscent
of Munch's work,
whose "bold colour-
symphonies" Leisti-
kow had defended
in late 1892 in the
journal *Freie Bühne*
(Free Stage) im-
mediately after the
exhibition scandal
that had greeted the
former's work.
Leistikow's *Lake
Grunewald* shows
the artist at his best. He avoids the
decorative simplification of some of
his works and goes far beyond merely
illustrating a topographically identifiable
location.   *AW*

Lovis Corinth   (1858–1925)

The Family of the Painter
Fritz Rumpf, 1901
Oil on canvas, 44 1/2 x 55 in.
Acquired 1927

Corinth painted this portrait of his
friend's family shortly after his return to
Berlin. There is no narrative linking the
figures, who should be seen as separate
individuals. They are held together by
the picture's colour composition and the
play of light, which ultimately creates an
unrealistic effect. Thus the shadowy pro-

files against the light on the left are contradicted by the brightly-lit mass of colour of the two younger children. These figures release a burst of colour that runs through the entire spectrum of reds and comes to rest in the orange-red of the blouse worn by the mother, which also halts the forward movement of the figures entering the scene from the left. The white of the large window with its rectangular panes is echoed in the shirt of a seated boy who is balanced by the puzzling, shadowy figure of a boy with a parrot in the lower right-hand corner. The brushwork, which no longer has anything to do with the actual depiction of objects, and the contrasts of light and shade that are here dissolved in colour, unite the figures in an on-going process that transcends any contingent spatial configurations and becomes a metaphor for the inner workings of the mind.   *AB*

Lovis Corinth   (1858–1925)

"Donna gravida," 1909
Oil on canvas, 37 ½ x 31 in.
Acquired 1916

This portrait of Corinth's pregnant wife is one of a long series of portraits of Charlotte Berend as lover, wife, mother, in allegorical costume, or playing a character part. In this work, which represents a rejection of both salon painting and formulaic pathos, Corinth, by now a successful portraitist of Berlin society, goes far beyond the spontaneous impression of what the eye sees. The theme of this portrait is the sitter's "physical self," expressed by a whole variety of means: the woman's head inclined gently to the left with questioning eyes and an open mouth, her expansive yet blurred physicality, the open blouse revealing the delicate flesh tint of her breasts, the fact that her clothes are echoed in the curtain in the background, the tender allusion of her position, and lastly, the interplay of her hands, one limp and one holding her clothes, which lends the whole an air of resolution. The sensitivity with which Corinth portrays the female form in this condition places him firmly among the leading portraitists of his day. This was the first work by Corinth that Ludwig Justi acquired for the Nationalgalerie in 1916.   *AB*

during a holiday on the Italian Riviera. It is fascinating for the immediacy of the angled, low viewpoint the artist has chosen despite the way that this distorts the features. The rose-decorated hat takes up the movement of the head and the eyes and sends it out elliptically beyond the picture edges. The expressive brushwork that seems to skim over the physicality of the décolleté is at its most powerful around the woman's eyes. With its inherent light, the colour in this work creates a feeling of vitality that banishes any threat of darkness.   *AB*

Lovis Corinth   (1858–1925)

Woman in Hat with Roses, 1912
Oil on canvas, 26³/₄ x 19³/₄ in.
Acquired 1952

This was one of the first pictures
Corinth painted after suffering a stroke

Max Slevogt   (1868–1932)

The Singer Francisco
d'Andrade as Don Giovanni in
Mozart's Opera (The Red d'Andrade),
1912
Oil on canvas, 82³/₄ x 67 in.
Acquired 1913

This portrait marked d'Andrade's thirtieth year on the stage. It shows the moment in the graveyard when Don Giovanni invites the statue of the Commendatore to supper. Ten years previously, Slevogt had painted a "White d'Andrade," which had received immediate acclaim. Where portrait and character role had become one in the earlier work, the "Red d'Andrade" depicts a whole scene where the generous rhythm of the picture planes and the expressive use of colour lend the subject a somewhat disembodied, floating quality. *AB*

Lovis Corinth (1858–1925)

The Blinded Samson, 1912
Oil on canvas, 51 1/4 x 41 1/4 in.
Acquired 1980

The blinded figure rushes towards the viewer with a power that threatens to shatter the picture. Samson's terror is expressed in his heroic nakedness, embittered blood-streaked face, and hands that can smash stone. Since the Middle Ages, artists' imaginations had been set on fire by the notion of "God's Chosen One" who towered mightily above other human beings: as a prefiguration of Christ, as a counterpart to Hercules, and as an image of the tragedy of the hero who pays for his untrammeled sensuality with his eyesight. *The Blinded Samson* is Corinth's third and last treatment of this theme. As a reaction to the stroke which threatened the artist's life in December 1911, it steps completely outside the traditional boundaries of its genre and finally shakes off the spell cast by the earlier example of Rembrandt. In this vision of the impending act of breaking free, which will destroy both Samson and his enemies, the painting becomes a drama of life and death. *AB*

Lovis Corinth   (1858–1925)

Pieces of Armor in the Studio, 1918
Oil on canvas, 38 ¼ x 32 ¼ in.
Acquired 1992 with funds from a donation
by Dr. Otto and Ilse Augustin

Using a broad brushstroke and an expressive touch that breaks up the forms, Corinth hurls down several pieces of armour, all rusty and smashed up. As a metaphor for fighting a losing battle they must have appeared fraught with significance, not only at the time, during the last years of World War I. Moreover, by questioning the limited effectiveness of any kind of armour — even in a figurative sense — they make an irritating impression. Nevertheless, Lovis Corinth, sixty years old and knowing a lot about life, does not interpret his motif — apparently found by chance, but this is actually one of a series of similar paintings of armour — in a superficial illustrative way, for instance as a metaphor for the experience of war or as a symbol of personal failure. Rather, he treats the Gary metallic surface enormously rich in colour reflections and nuances primarily as a problem of painting technique. He traces the rounded forms with paint, plays with sparkling lights and shadows, and crowns the picture, which disintegrates vaguely before the viewer's eyes, with blood-red colour highlights in the distance.   *BM*

Max Beckmann   (1884–1950)

Conversation, 1908
Oil on canvas, 69 ¾ x 66 ½ in.
Acquired 1963 with funds from the
German Lottery Foundation

Beckmann looks out from the shadows of the background at his pregnant wife standing in the center, her mother, who is seated, and his sister, standing on the right. The isolation of the individual figures prevents this from being a conversation piece, making it instead into a strongly lit pantomime with lead parts and minor parts. This conversation is like a counterpart to Beckmann's death scene of 1906 but, because of the different ages of the protagonists, may also be an allusion to the traditional iconography of the "ages of man." This would explain the thoughtful look on the mother's face; perhaps she is reflecting on birth and death. This existential dimension and the tense composition of spaces and areas of concentration were later to become characteristic of Max Beckmann's work.   *BM*

Max Beckmann (1884–1950)

Small Death Scene, 1906
Oil on canvas, 43 ¼ x 28 in.
Acquired 1952

Paralyzed by the incomprehensibility of death, the mourners have gathered in the anteroom, pale, disconnected, somberly dressed. The deathbed stands in the next room, and it is only there that the gestures of grief are evident. In 1906, Beckmann's mother died. With the two works *Birth* and *Death* (1936–37, in the Neue Nationalgalerie), Beckmann was again to return to the basic questions of human existence, but in a much more modern manner. Perhaps death here might also symbolically be that of the nineteenth century itself. Although this work brings the tour of the Alte Nationalgalerie to a close, the story is taken up again by the modern classics of Munch and the Expressionists in the Neue Nationalgalerie. *BM*

Bibliography

Max Jordan, *Beschreibendes Verzeichnis der Kunstwerke in der Königlichen National-Galerie zu Berlin*, Berlin 1876 (and later editions)

Ausstellung deutscher Kunst aus der Zeit von 1775–1875 in der Königlichen Nationalgalerie, Berlin, vol. 1–2, Berlin 1906

(Hugo von Tschudi) *Verzeichnis der Gemälde und Skulpturen in der Königlichen National-Galerie zu Berlin*, Berlin 1908 (and later editions)

Ludwig Justi, *Deutsche Malkunst im neunzehnten Jahrhundert. Ein Führer durch die Nationalgalerie*, Berlin 1920

Paul Ortwin Rave, *Das Schinkel-Museum und die Kunst-Sammlungen Beuths*, Berlin 1931

Paul Ortwin Rave, *Das Rauch-Museum in der Orangerie des Charlottenburger Schlosses*, Berlin 1930

Kurt Karl Eberlein, *Vorgeschichte und Entstehung der Nationalgalerie*, in: *Jahrbuch der Preußischen Kunstsammlungen 51*, 1930, pp. 250–61

Paul Ortwin Rave, *Die Geschichte der Nationalgalerie*, Berlin 1968

Verzeichnis der Gemälde und Skulpturen des 19. Jahrhunderts, Nationalgalerie Berlin, Staatliche Museen Preußischer Kulturbesitz, Berlin 1976

Claude Keisch, *Die Sammlung Wagener. Aus der Vorgeschichte der Nationalgalerie*, Berlin 1976

Dieter Honisch, *Die Nationalgalerie Berlin*, Recklinghausen 1979

Staatliche Museen zu Berlin, Nationalgalerie. *Die Gemälde der Nationalgalerie, Verzeichnis: Deutsche Malerei vom Klassizismus bis zum Impressionismus, Ausländische Malerei von 1800 bis 1930*, Berlin 1986

Christopher With, *The Prussian Landeskunstkommission 1862–1911. A Study in State Subvention of the Arts*, Berlin 1986

Peter Krieger, *Galerie der Romantik. Nationalgalerie*, Berlin 1986

Jörn Grabowski, *Die politische und kunstpolitische Konzeption der Nationalgalerie, behandelt anhand der Erwerbungen historischer Darstellungen 1861–1896*, Berlin 1990

Jörn Grabowski, *Die Neue Abteilung der Nationalgalerie im ehemaligen Kronprinzen-Palais*, in: *Jahrbuch Preußischer Kulturbesitz 28*, 1991, pp. 341–57

Barbara Paul, *Hugo von Tschudi und die moderne französische Kunst im Deutschen Kaiserreich*, Mainz 1993

Robert Graefrath, Bernhard Maaz, *Die Friedrichswerdersche Kirche in Berlin. Baudenkmal und Museum*, Berlin 1993

Jörn Grabowski, *Die Nationale Bildnis-Sammlung. Zur Geschichte der ersten Nebenabteilung der Nationalgalerie*, in: *Jahrbuch Preußischer Kulturbesitz 31*, 1994, pp. 297–322

Johann Georg Prinz von Hohenzollern, Peter-Klaus Schuster (Eds.), *Manet bis van Gogh. Hugo von Tschudi und der Kampf um die Moderne*, Berlin/Munich 1996

Hartmut Dorgerloh, *Die Nationalgalerie. Zur Geschichte des Gebäudes auf der Museumsinsel 1841–1970*, Berlin 1997

Claudia Rückert, Sven Kuhrau (Eds.), *"Der Deutschen Kunst". Nationalgalerie und nationale Identität 1876–1998*, Dresden 1998

Bernhard Maaz, *Alte Nationalgalerie (in: Berliner Ansichten)*, Berlin 1999

Nationalgalerie. *Gesamtverzeichnis der Gemälde und Skulpturen*. Staatliche Museen zu Berlin, CD-ROM, Berlin 2001

List of Artists

Third Exhibition Level

3.01   Schadow and Art around 1800
3.02   Murals from Casa Bartholdy
3.03, 3.04   The Goethe Period
3.05   Karl Friedrich Schinkel
3.06   Caspar David Friedrich
3.07   Carl Blechen
3.08–3.13   Romanticism, Biedermeier, Düsseldorf School
3.14   Nazarenes
3.15   Peter Cornelius, Cartoons

Second Exhibition Level

2.01   Neo-Baroque Sculptures
2.02   The German-Romans
2.03   French Impressionists
2.04   Temporary Exhibitions
2.05, 2.06   The German-Romans
2.07, 2.08   Wilhelm Leibl and his Circle
2.09–2.12   Realism in Germany
2.13   Max Liebermann, Fritz von Uhde
2.14   Munich Painting
2.15   History Painting and Salon Idealism

First Exhibition Level

1.01   Neoclassical Sculpture
1.02, 1.03   Realism from Constable to Courbet
1.04   Realism in Germany and Austria
1.04a   History of the Nationalgalerie
1.05   Adolph Menzel
1.06   Adolph Menzel, Franz Krüger
1.07   Temporary Exhibitions
1.08–1.12   Adolph Menzel
1.13, 1.14   Art around 1900 in Europe
1.15, 1.16   Secessions and Art at the Turn of the Century

Lower Level

Museum Shop
Espresso Bar
Information
W.C.
Handicapped Access